COL SPORCAR SI TROVA

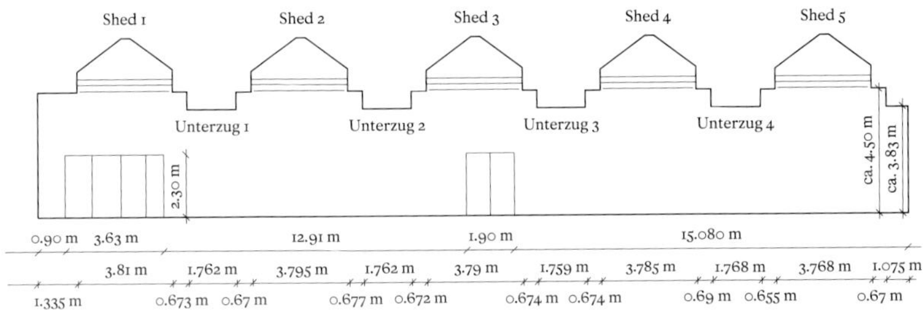

Shed 1
Shed 2
Shed 3
Shed 4
Shed 5
Unterzug 1
Unterzug 2
Unterzug 3
Unterzug 4
2.30 m
ca. 4.50 m
ca. 3.83 m
0.90 m
3.63 m
12.91 m
1.90 m
15.080 m
3.81 m
1.762 m
3.795 m
1.762 m
3.79 m
1.759 m
3.785 m
1.768 m
3.768 m
1.075 m
1.335 m
0.673 m
0.67 m
0.677 m
0.672 m
0.674 m
0.674 m
0.69 m
0.655 m
0.67 m

Kathrin Bentele (ed.)

Yuki Kimura

COL SPORCAR SI TROVA

Kunstverein für die
Rheinlande und Westfalen
Düsseldorf

Mousse Publishing

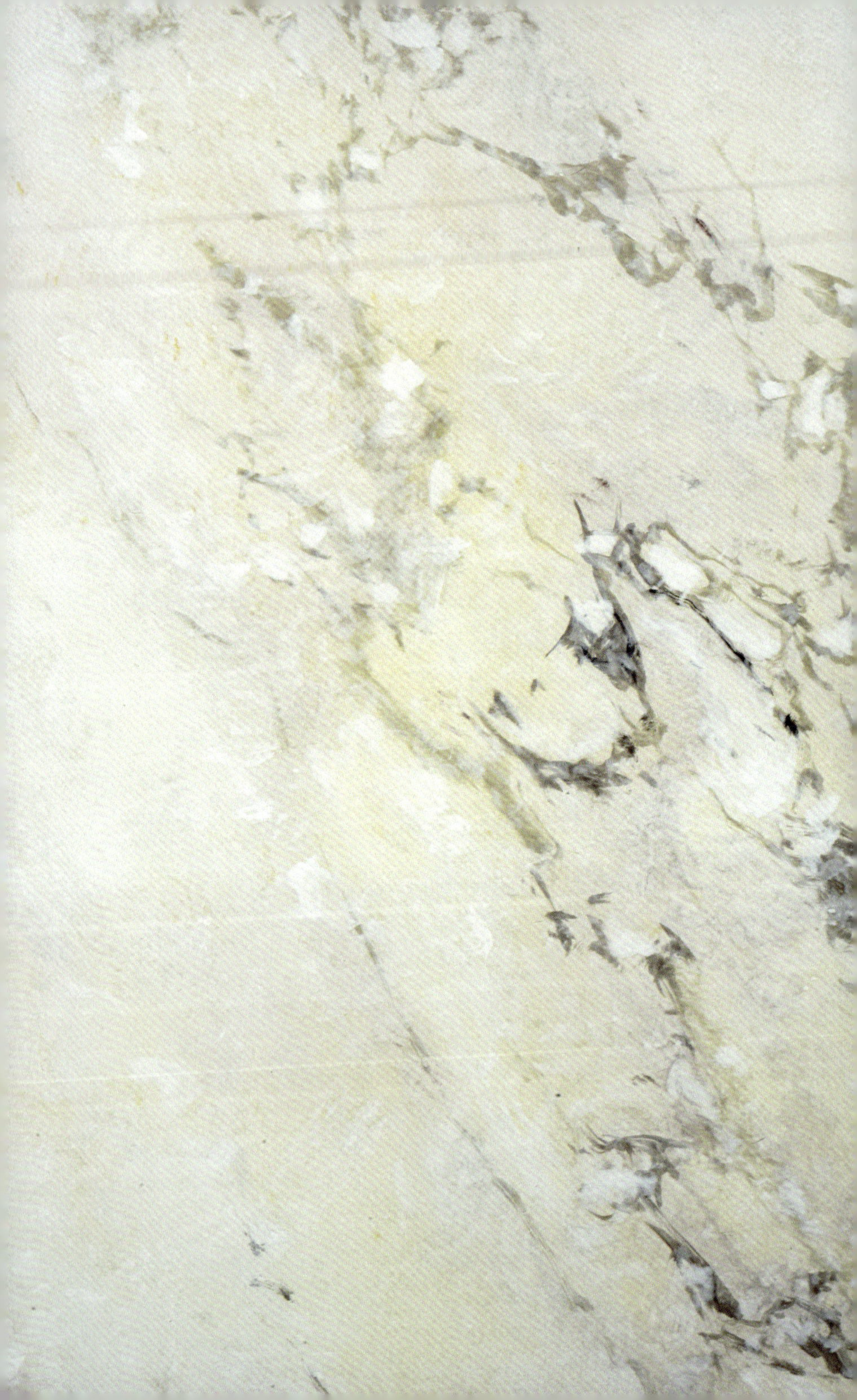

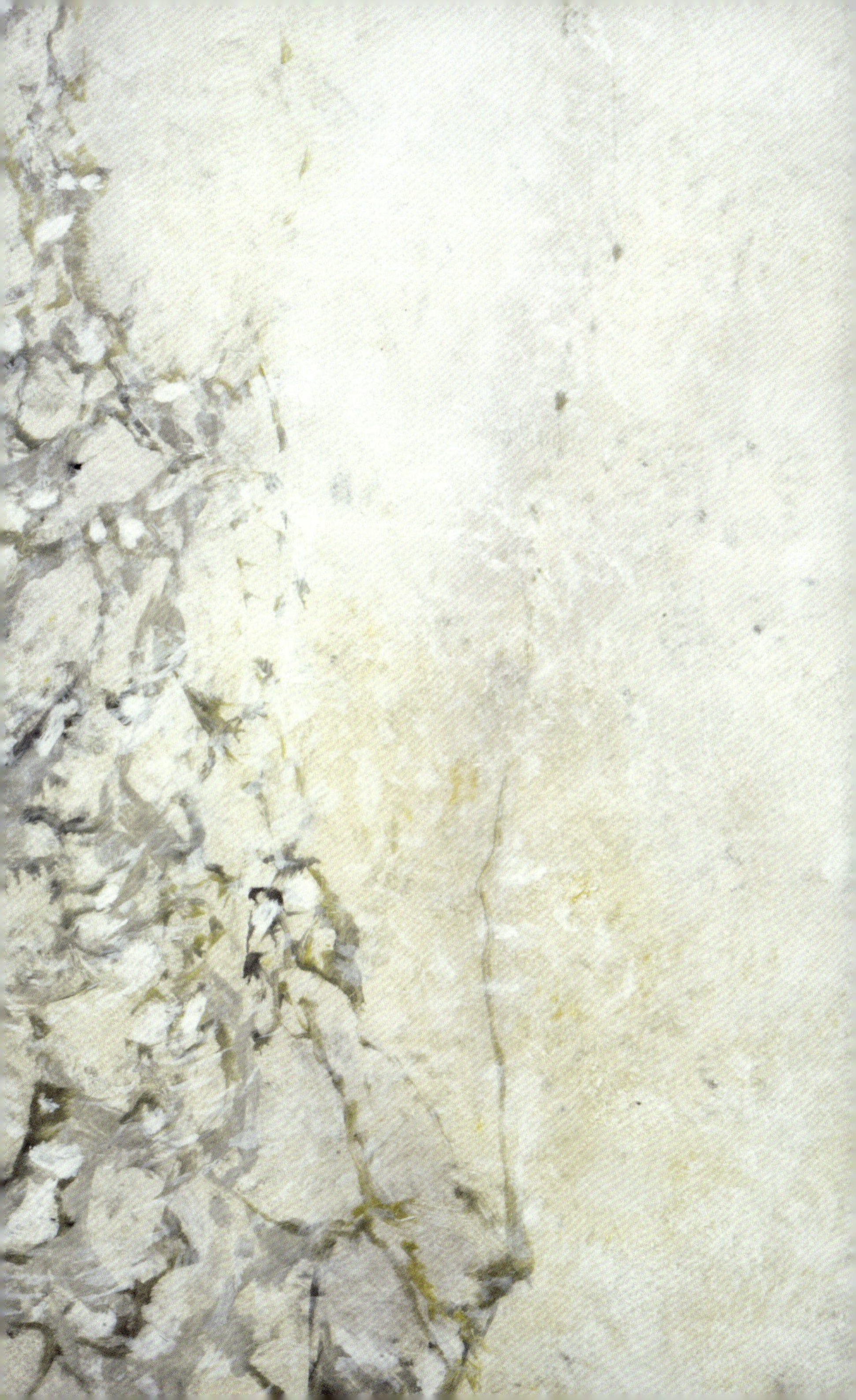

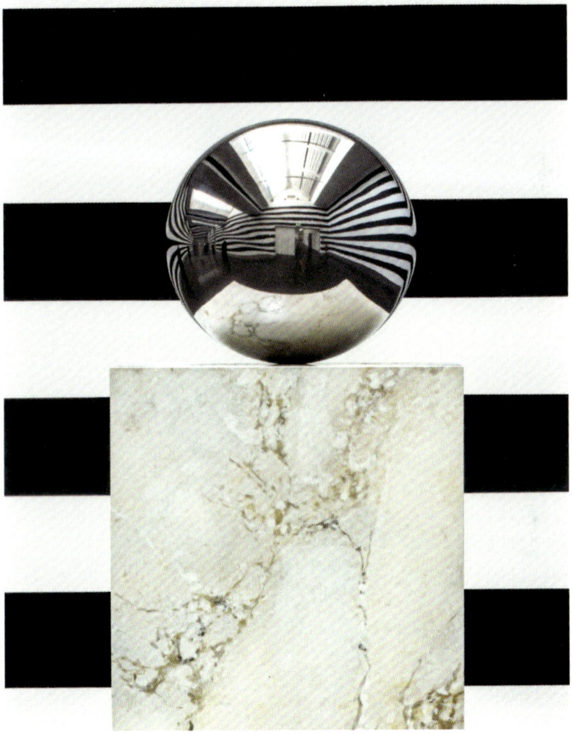

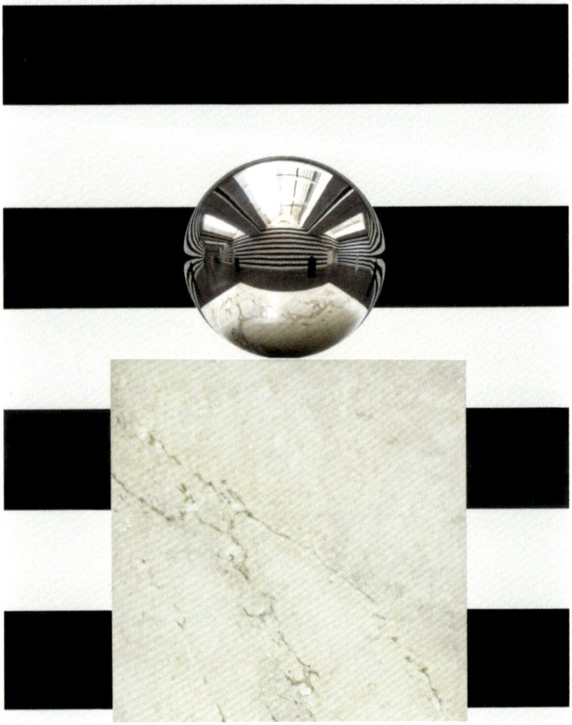

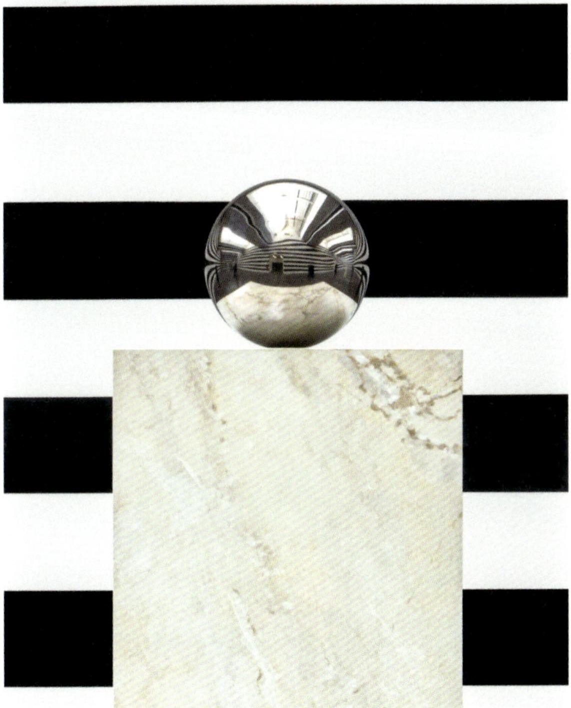

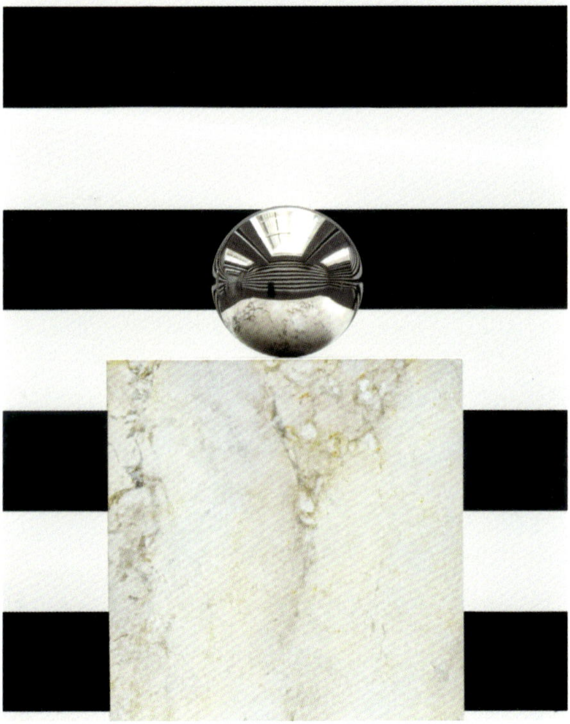

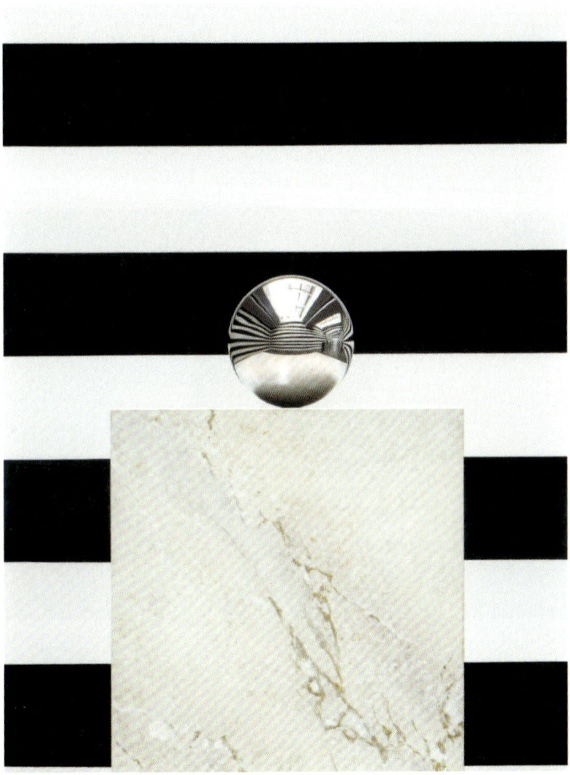

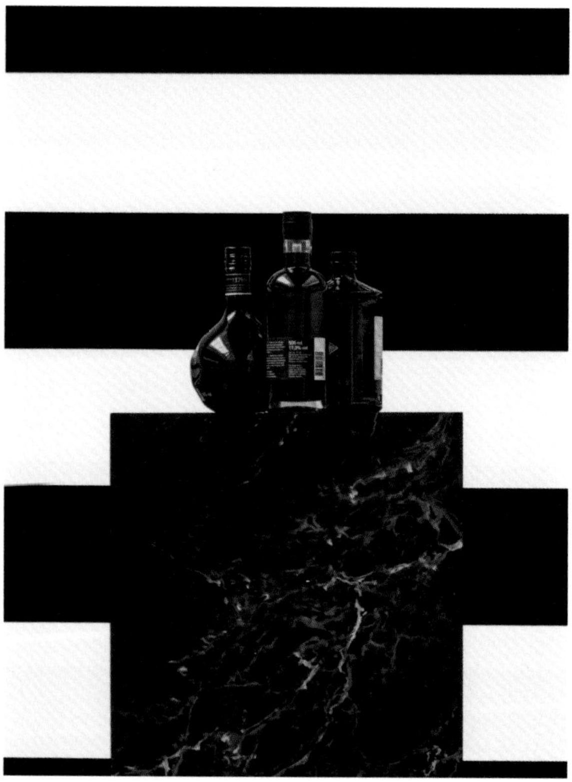

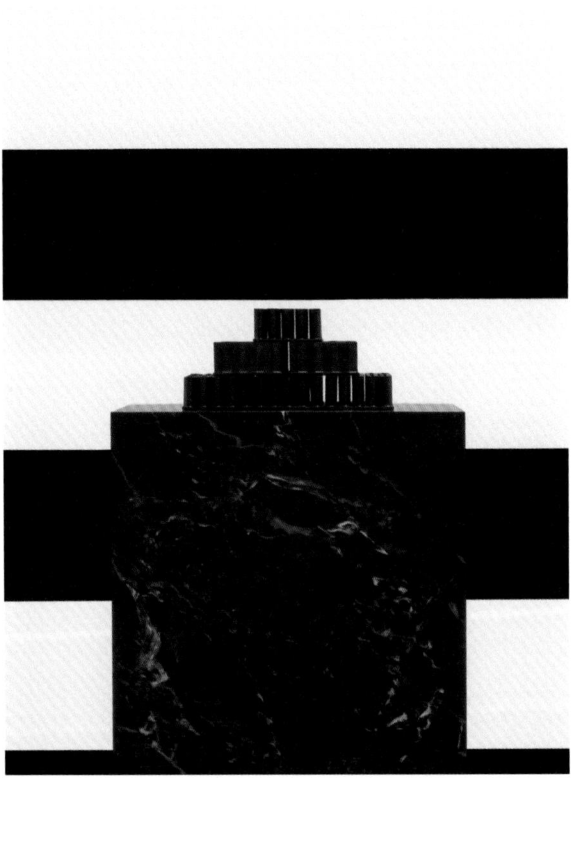

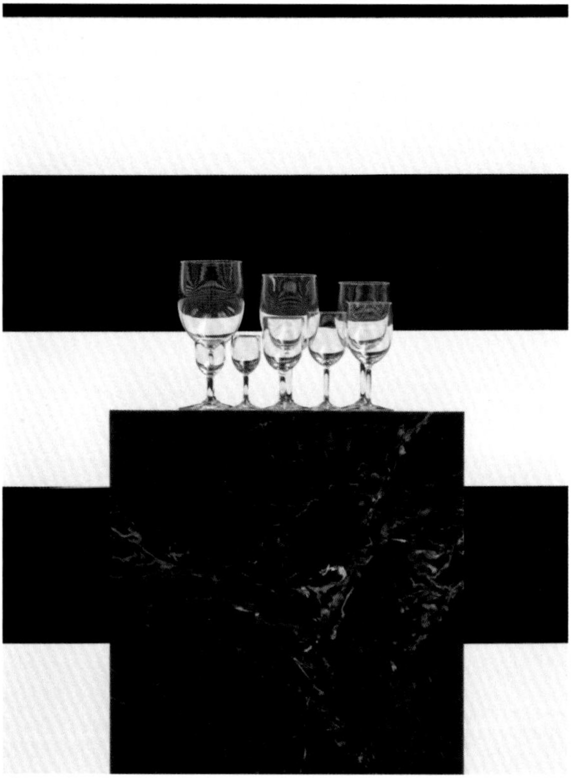

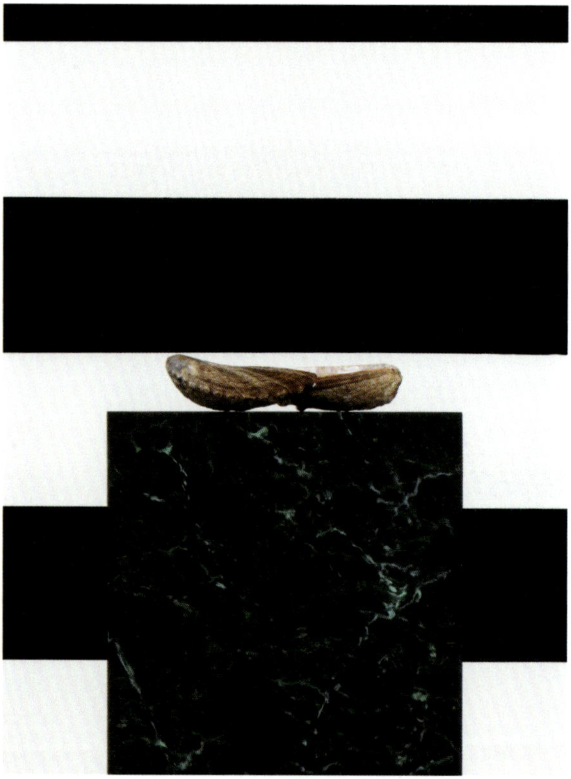

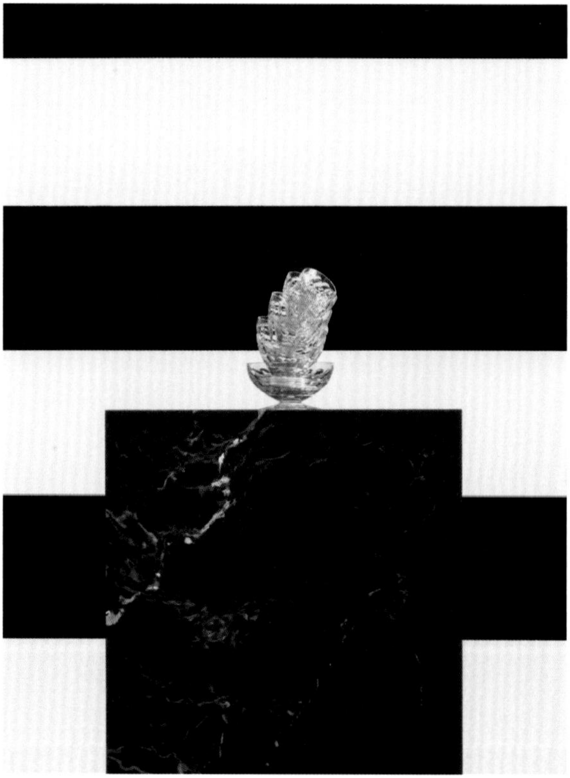

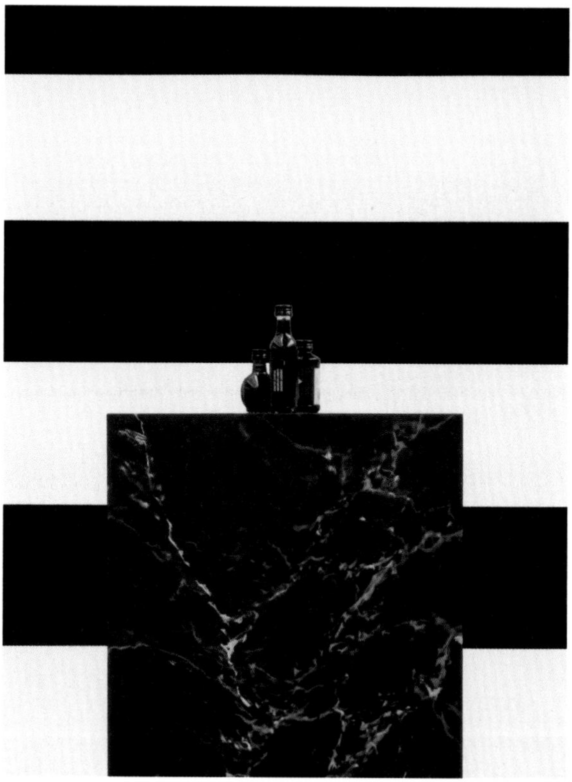

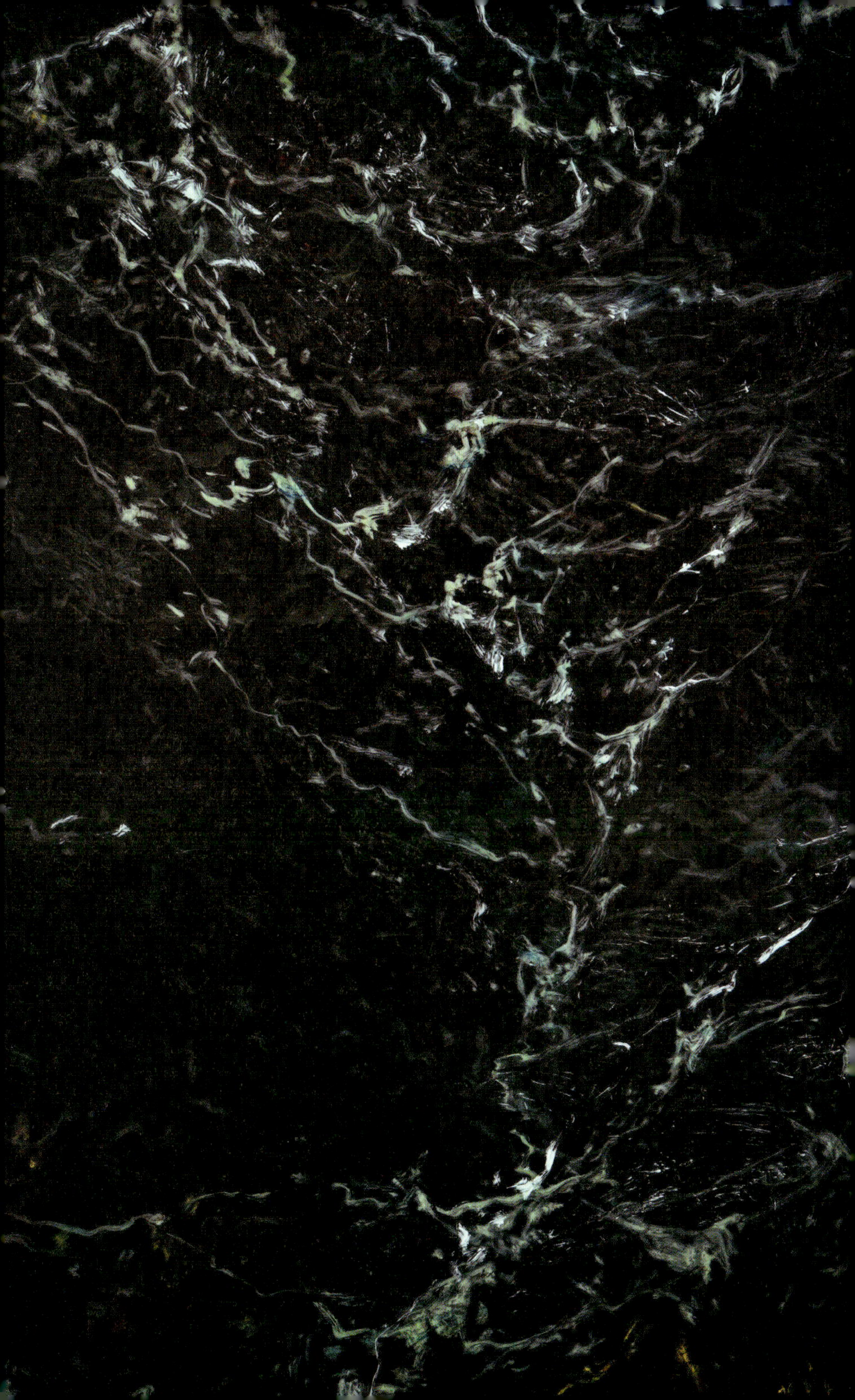

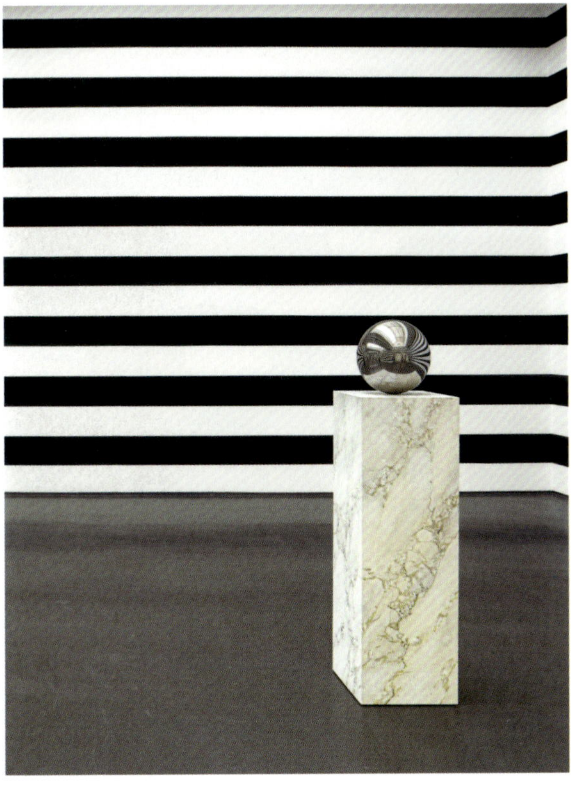

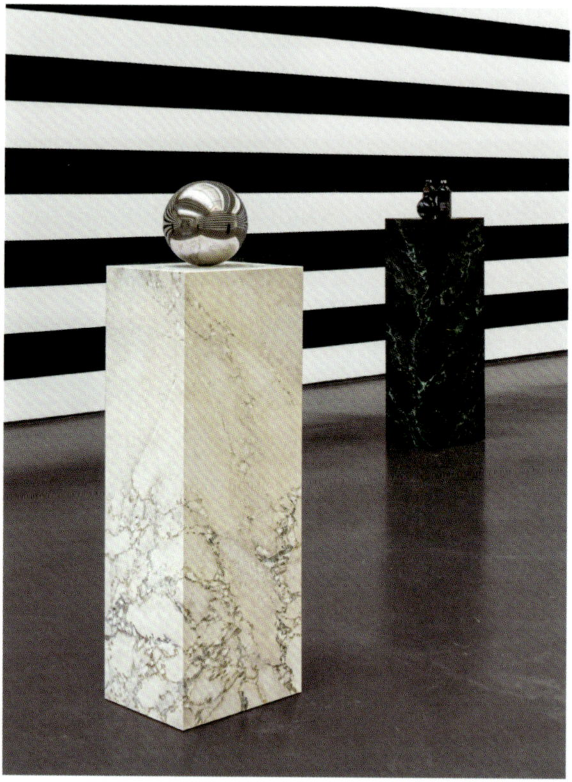

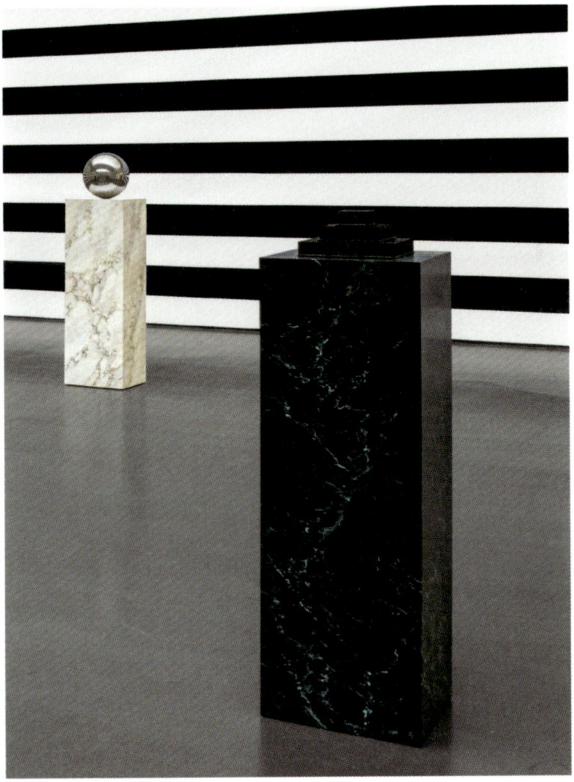

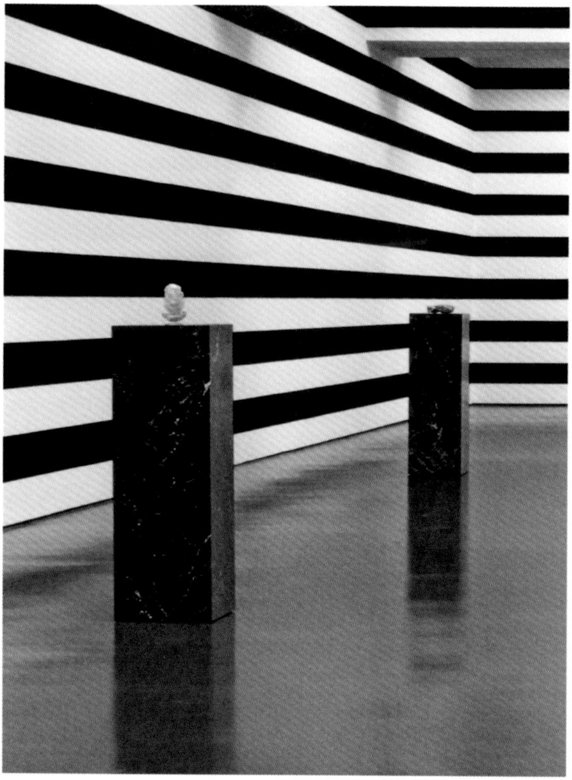

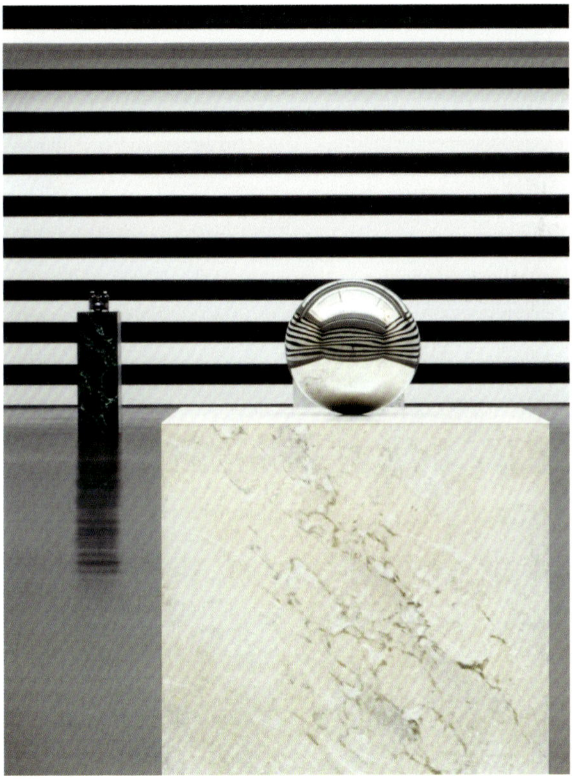

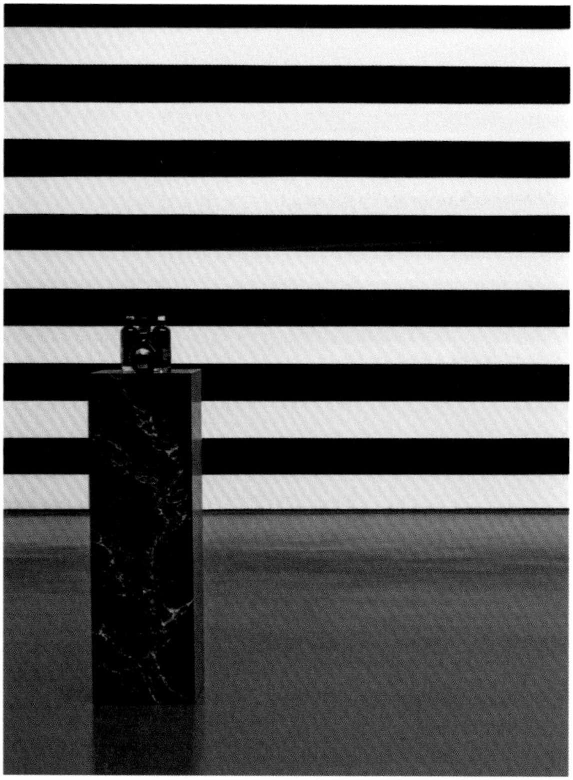

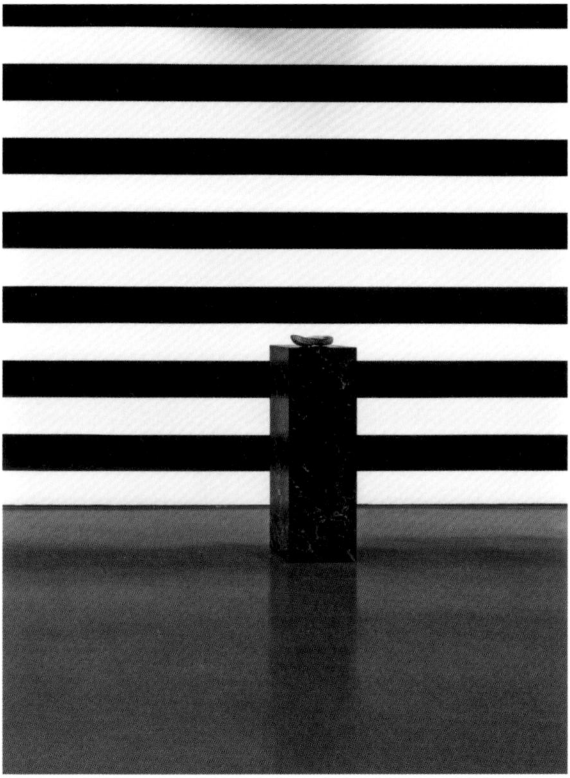

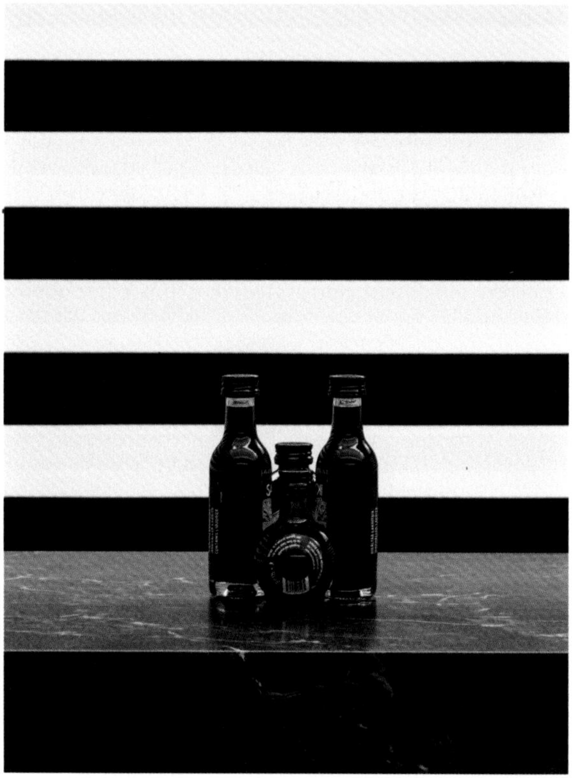

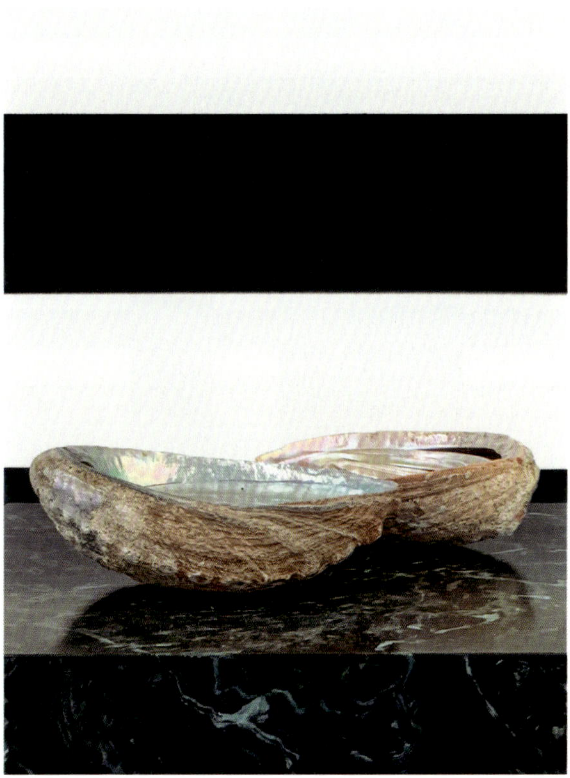

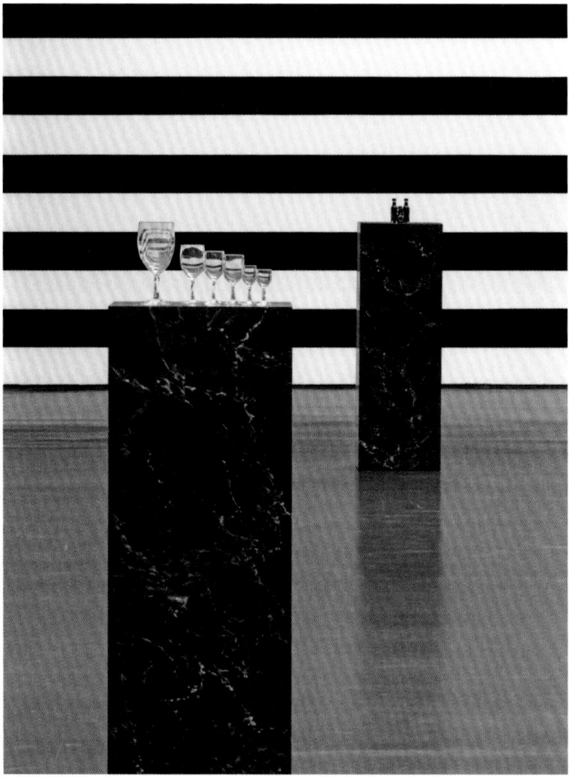

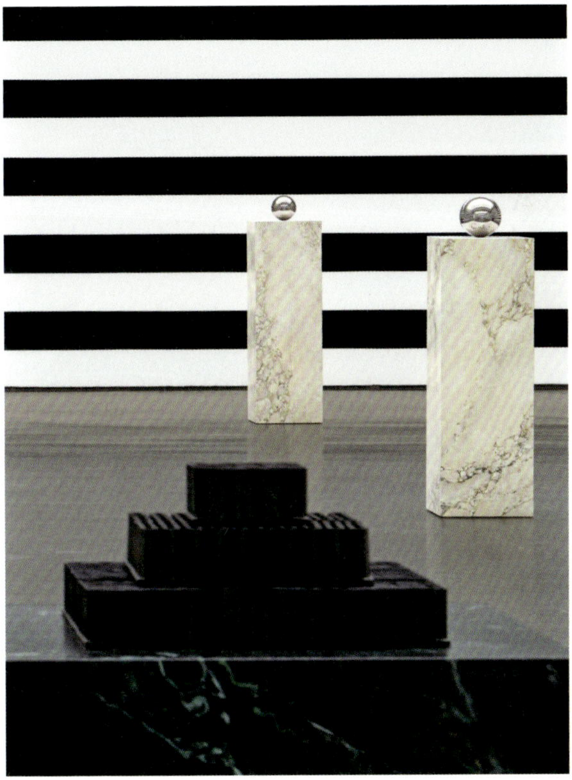

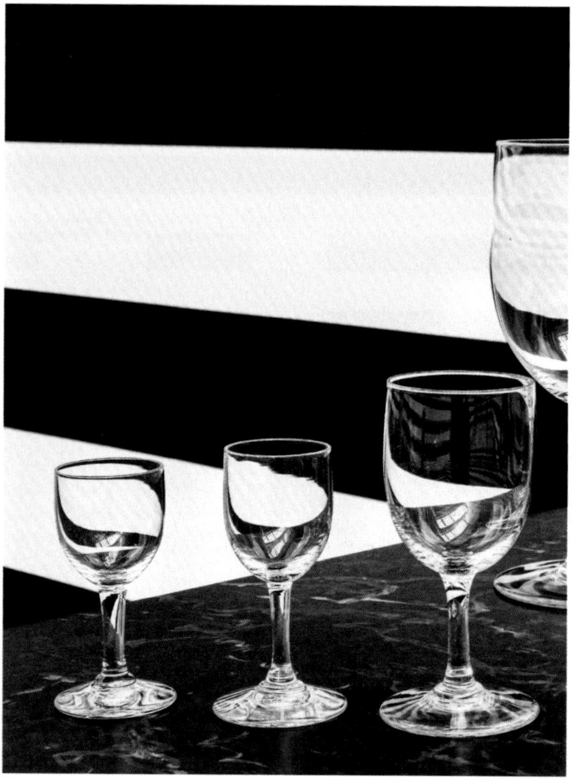

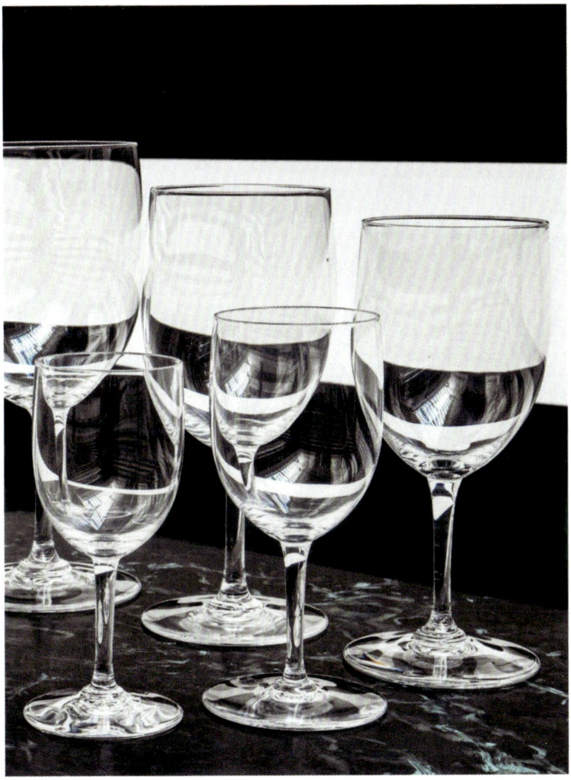

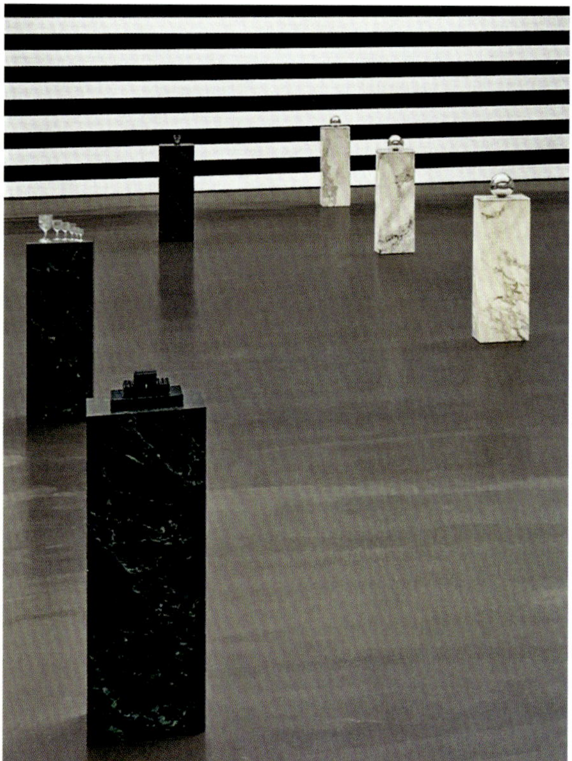

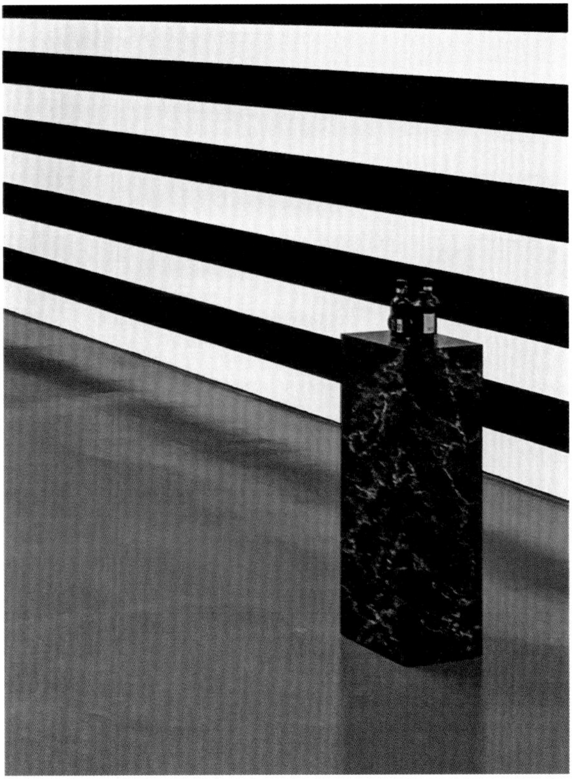

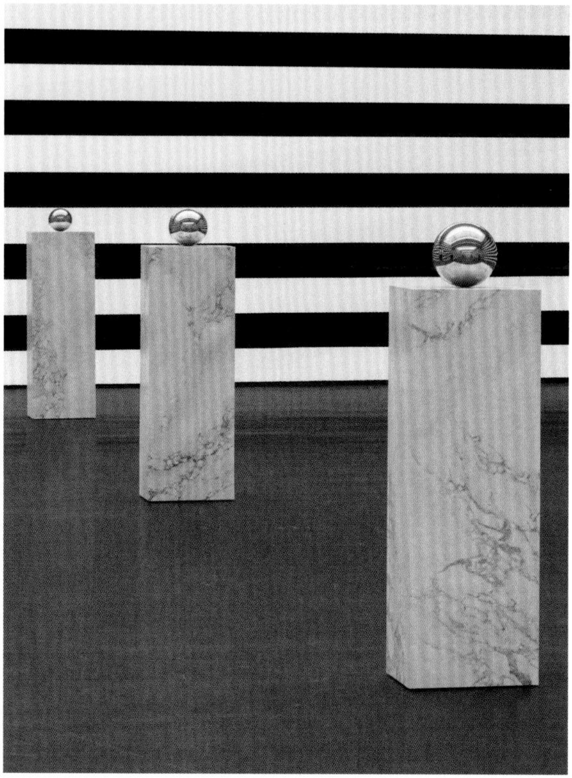

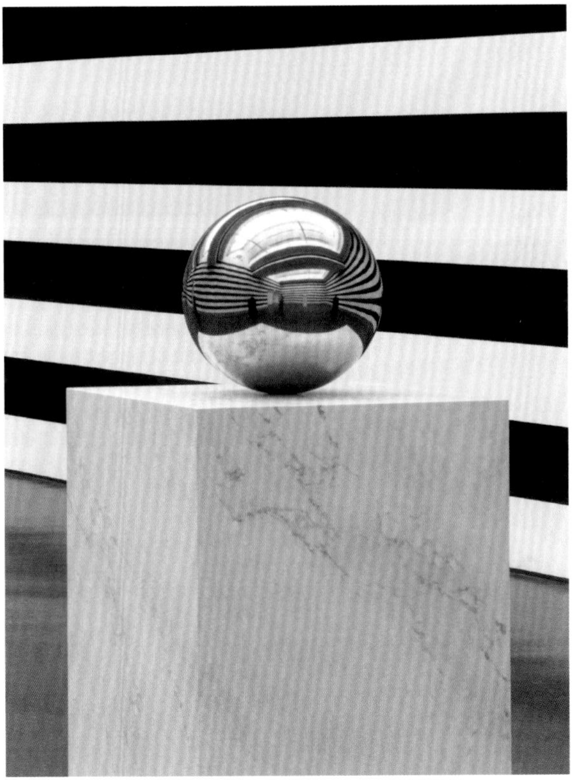

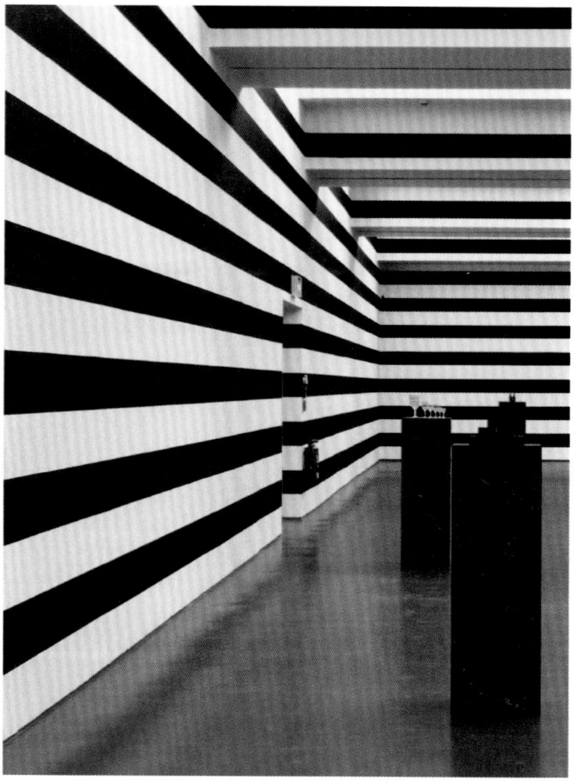

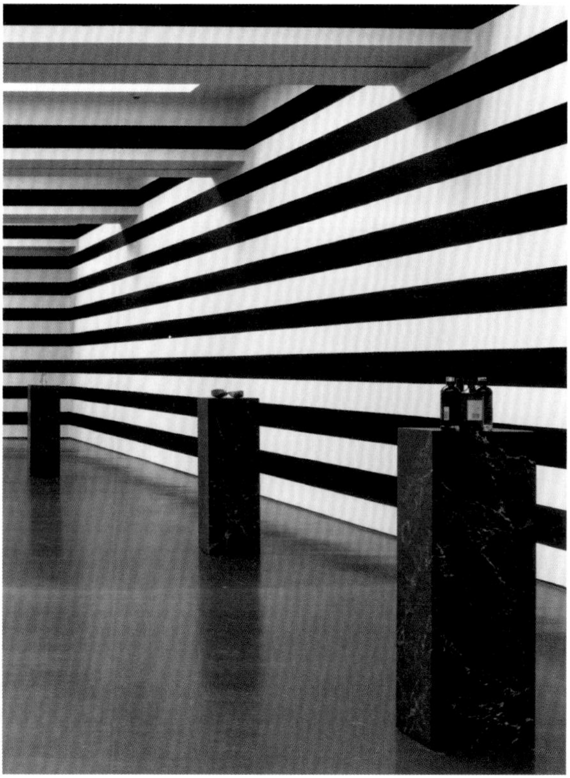

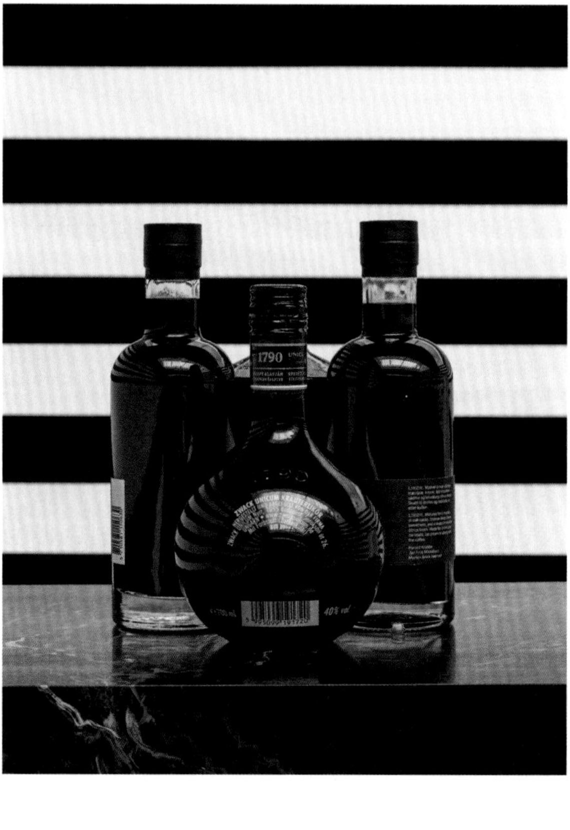
1790
40% vol

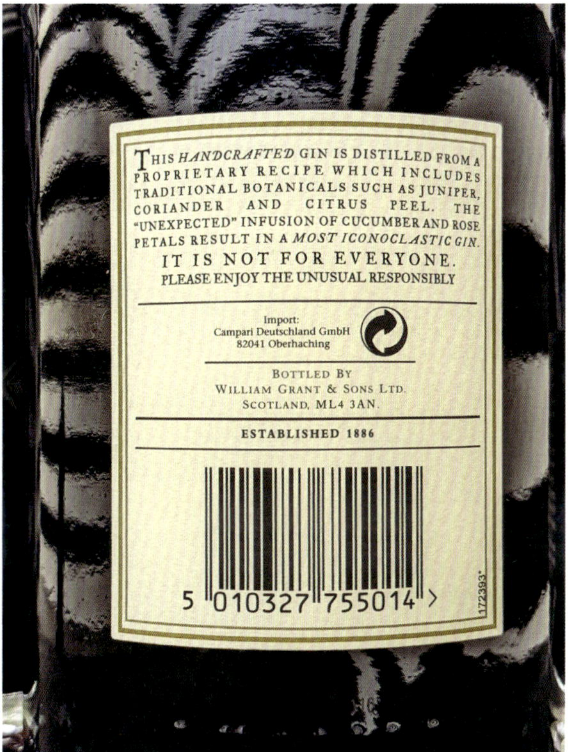
THIS *HANDCRAFTED* GIN IS DISTILLED FROM A PROPRIETARY RECIPE WHICH INCLUDES TRADITIONAL BOTANICALS SUCH AS JUNIPER, CORIANDER AND CITRUS PEEL. THE "UNEXPECTED" INFUSION OF CUCUMBER AND ROSE PETALS RESULT IN A *MOST ICONOCLASTIC GIN.*
IT IS NOT FOR EVERYONE.
PLEASE ENJOY THE UNUSUAL RESPONSIBLY
Import:
Campari Deutschland GmbH
82041 Oberhaching
BOTTLED BY
WILLIAM GRANT & SONS LTD.
SCOTLAND, ML4 3AN.
ESTABLISHED 1886
5 010327 755014
172393*

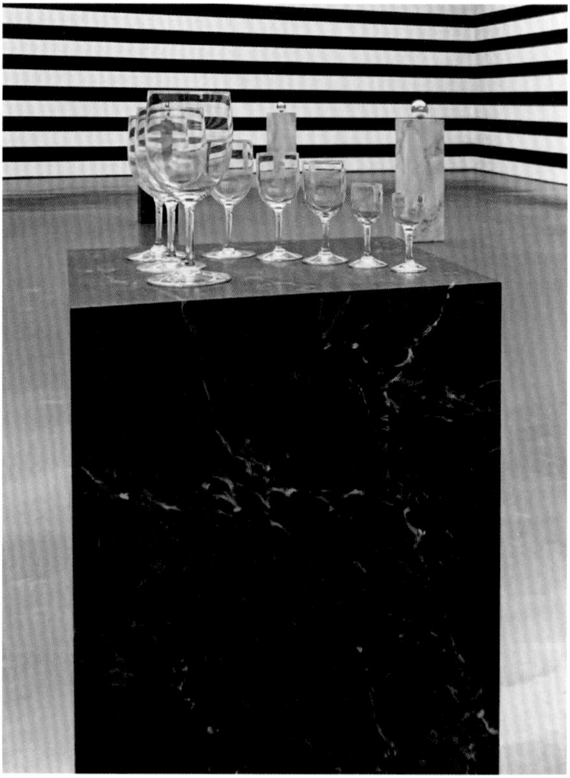

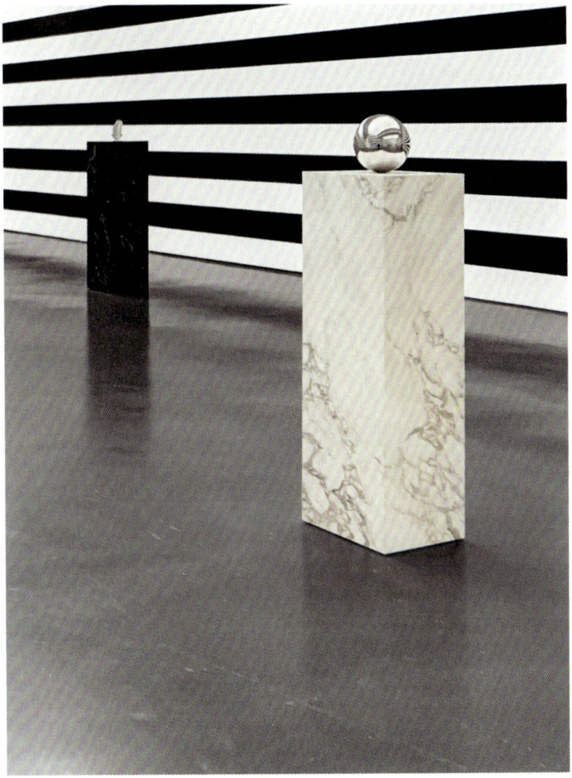

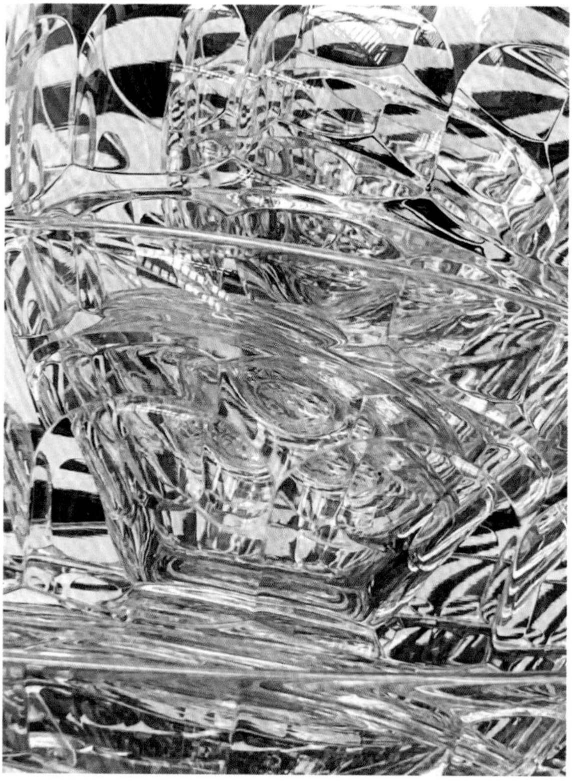

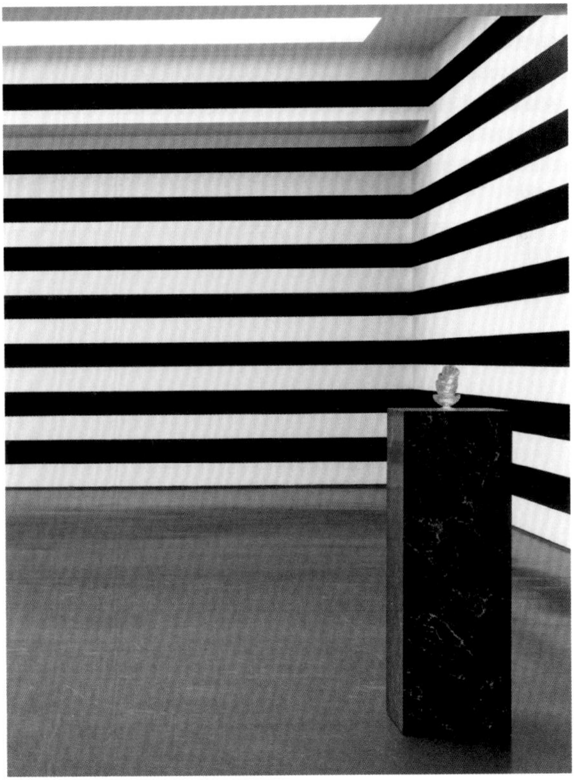

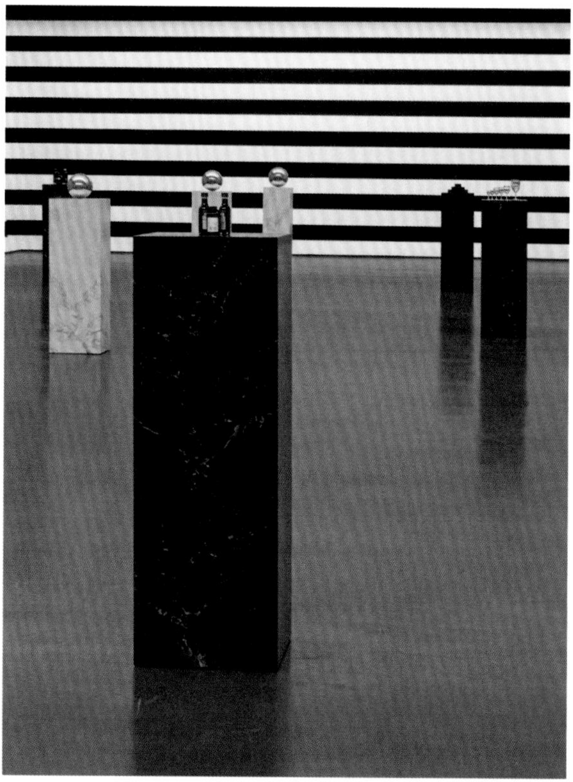

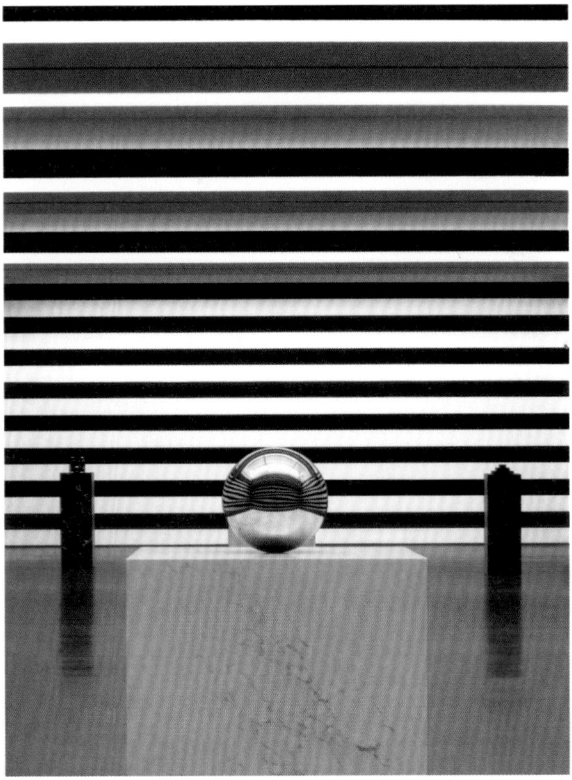

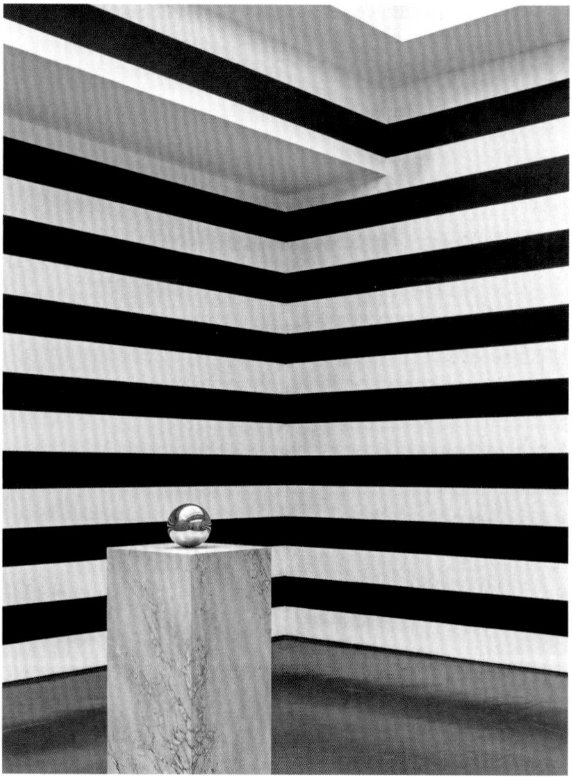

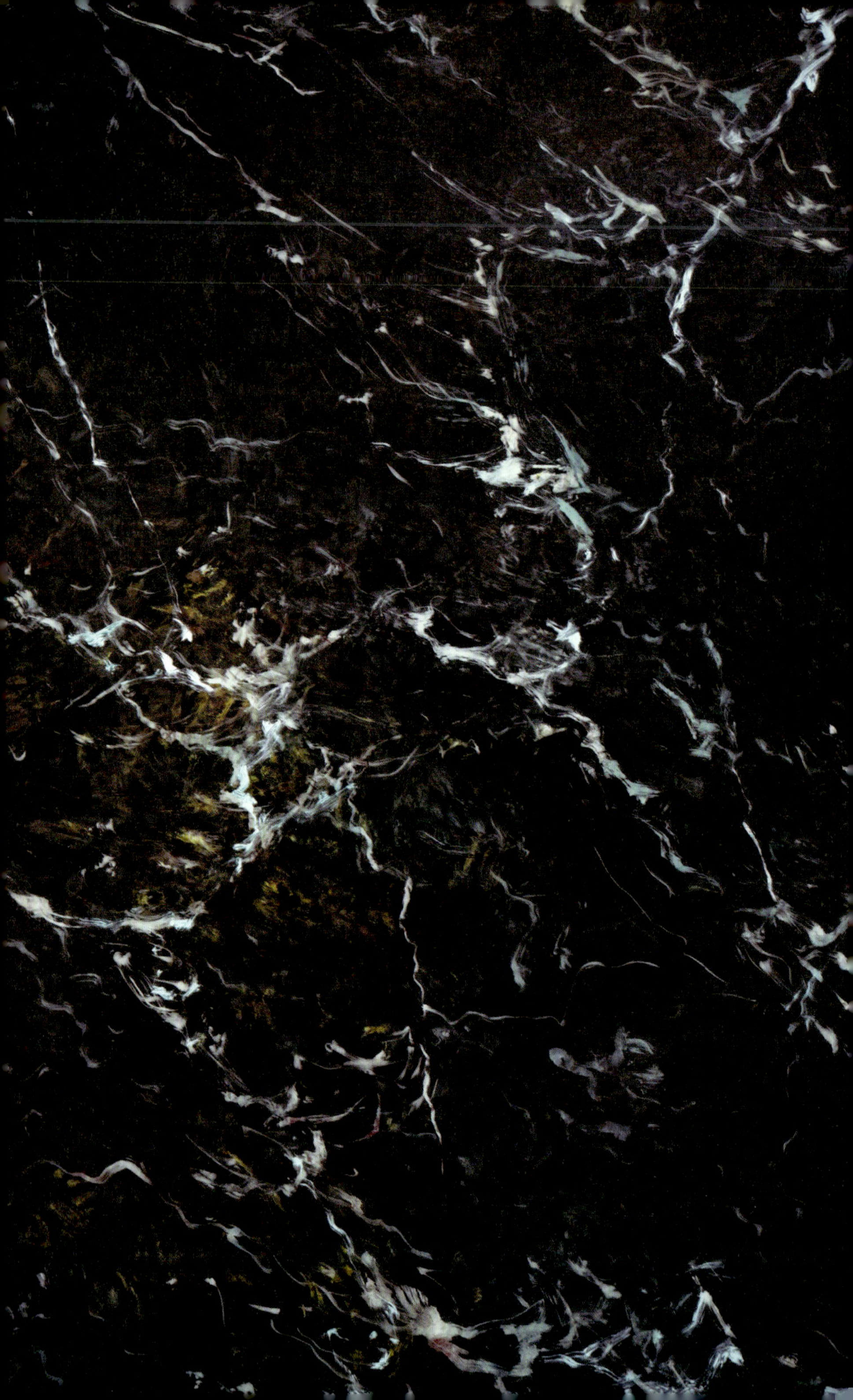

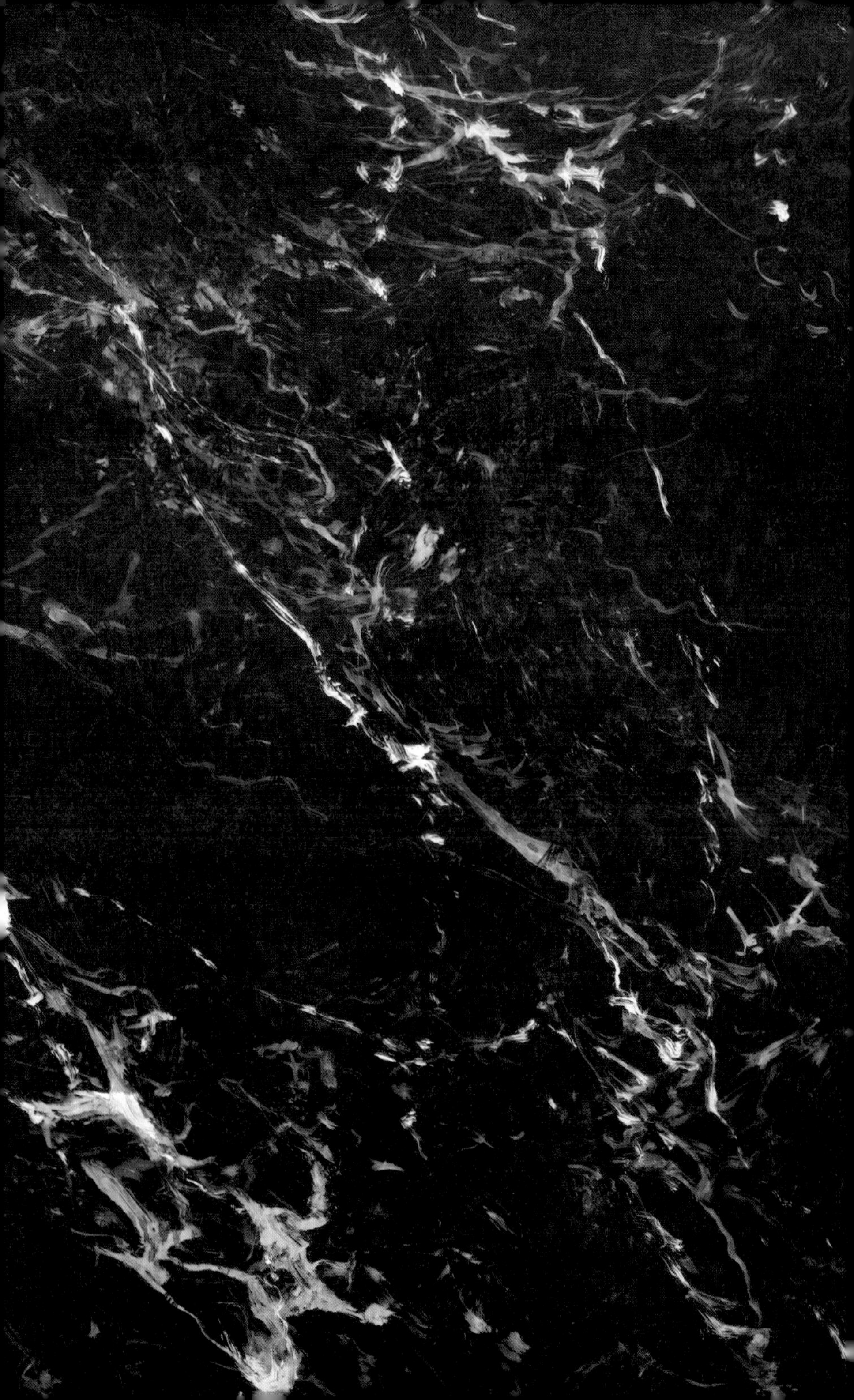

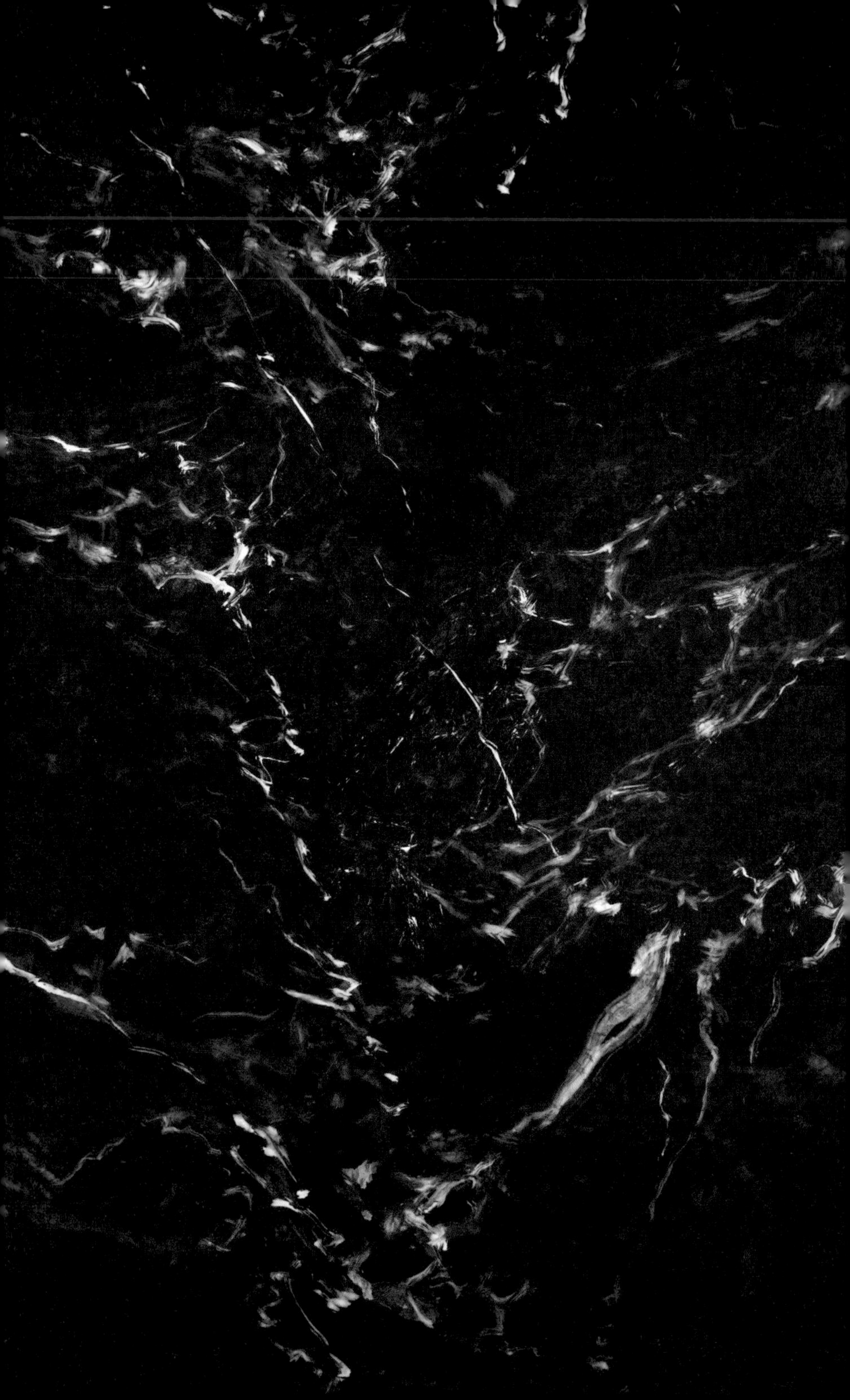

Jamie Stevens

WITHIN AND WITHOUT

Entering the building, I wondered about the particular challenge of the Kunstverein being nested within a larger building that contains another institution. I imagined the subtle boundary-making efforts that Kathrin Bentele and the staff of the Kunstverein probably put in place, some quietly fought battle of fault lines and distinctions in a necessarily collaborative cohabitation. "Right here for the Kunsthalle, next door on left for the Kunstverein." I have heard my flatmate tell friends that particular objects in our rented apartment belong to me, and I understand this as his clarification that certain things in our shared environment must be strictly attributed to me to save him from being misrepresented. I know that I do the same. Our indirect negotiations and compromises end where our bedrooms begin, a border beyond which each of our singular styles can be more fully elaborated. Visiting Yuki Kimura's show, the threshold of the gallery indeed marked a vivid borderline of a space that had been given a total formal treatment, and I wondered if this decision might have, in part, been mobilized by the enforced dialogue with institutional conditions beyond those controlled by only the Kunstverein. Or perhaps it was a sort of *joining* with the Kunstverein, creating a forcefully maintained

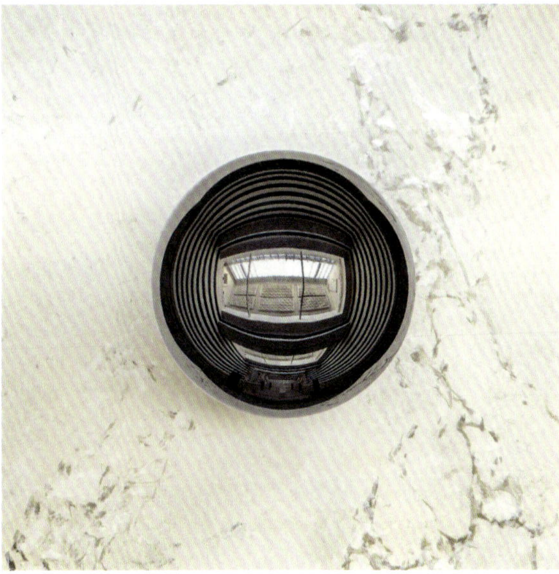

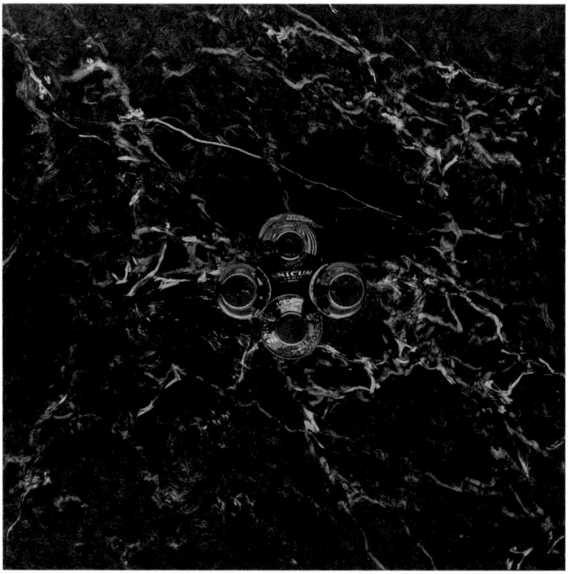
UNICUM

boundary—for both institution and artist—that could more directly and imaginatively mark a point of crossing for visitors.

At the beginning and end of my time in the main gallery were the wardrobe pieces, positioned by the window in the large reception area located in one of the mixed interstitial zones of the building. These had once been installed in Kimura's childhood bedroom in Kyoto. The timber surfaces of the wardrobes are scorched by sunlight at different intensities in a composition that implies their original position and use, but they are now dislocated from a room where the artist would have transitioned from childhood, through puberty, into young adulthood. Like the main exhibition hall, we are invited to make contact with a room of transformations.

As I stepped into the gallery, the exhibition quickly unspooled itself in a carefully organized way, with plinths descending along invisible pyramidic vectors, their objects growing or shrinking

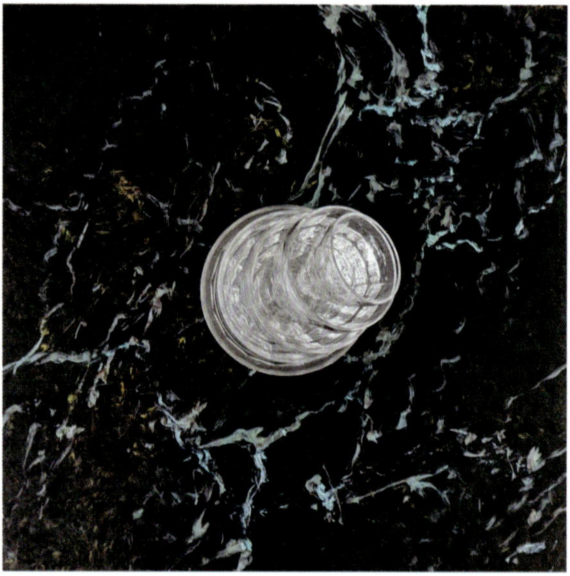

in incremental scales. This was an exhibition to perceive as a whole, and I felt a pressure to inhale it in one go. I found myself pressed by the works on display to engage an impossible task: I was to find some perfect place in the exhibition hall that could settle my vision into the distortions and illusions intended for the viewer. Now, however, I think this reflex to find the precise spot that could omnipotently calm the vibrating visual activity of Kimura's works was a product of my discomfort. Discomfort because I felt an oppressive quality to the stagecraft of the space, Kimura drenching the gallery with grids both visible and intangible, purging it of any vantage point for respite. In the world of high-fidelity audio, critics speak of seeking out sound, not music. Something of that nature is what I felt in pursuit of. There were crystalline frequencies present and aimed to a sweet spot of listening, from where the music would surely follow.

I once visited the courtyard of the Palazzo Spada in Rome with its beautiful architectural folly of a grand outdoor gallery of columns receding into the middle distance, framing a statue of Mars. In fact, Mars stands just 60 centimetres high, and the vaulted colonnade, although implying some 30 metres or more, is under 9 metres in length. A leaflet gave the meaning of the folly as an architectural joke for its patron, a fake expansion of the property line. I understood this explanation while looking at the folly but not because of its trickery and mastery of perspective. The operation of the joke seemed instead to be in installing a more fundamentally self-conscious presence to its environment. A lavish architectural gesture that was also an act of puncture. While I stood there, looking from the spot that activates the hallucination, a stray cat walked into the installation, but somehow the clash of scales did not harm the architectural illusion. It did, however, seem to distort the form of the cat. This experience was mirrored in some way by my visit to Kimura's exhibition. I was the figure that felt irregularly reconstituted in a hall of mirrors despite the static reality of things.

Indicative of Kimora's artistic idiom, the readymades on the plinths had a silent and unhurried quality. There is a strong and disarming

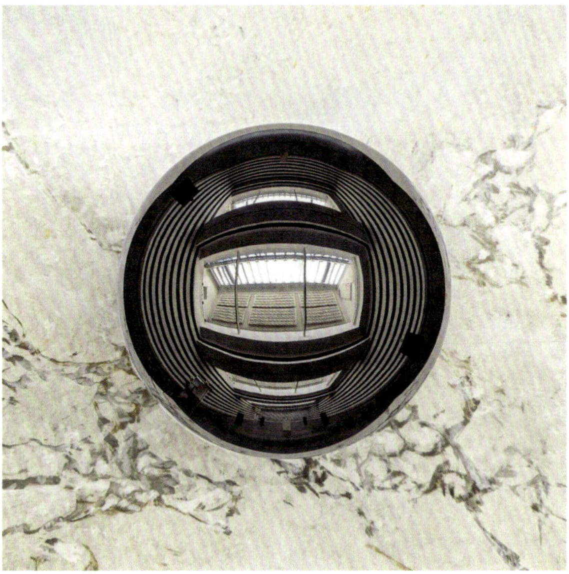

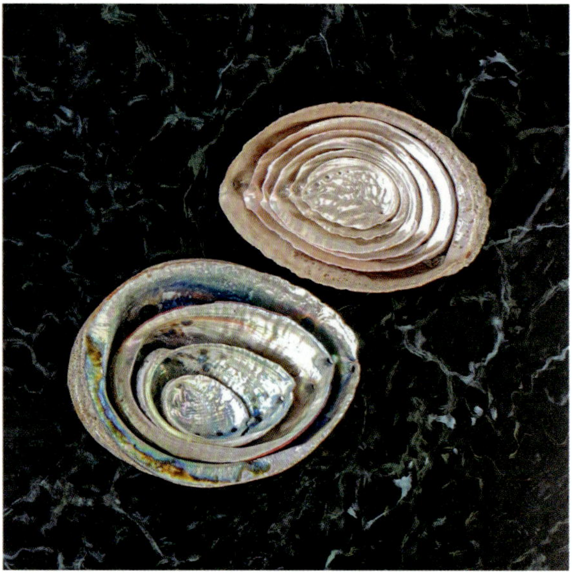

sense of something having been worked through outside of the presentation phase of the project, with little impulse to share the methods of the exhibition's creation. To my eyes, this lent the exhibition an unsettling authority, mute to its expected receptions and somehow staunch despite its delicate arrangement. Nevertheless, I attempted to create my own internal composition of the exhibition, to create links and associations that would orient my own mind in this space that offered no simple disclosures for how I was supposed to see it. The objects did share allusions to altered states: the vessels for pouring and drinking alcohol, the large abalone shells indicative of aphrodisiacs or apothecary, the empty pen pots a void in which the artist's most powerful tool can rest, and a mirrored surface that distorts its surrounding environment. I'm straining here, though, for something the exhibition refused to hand to me, namely an "about" that could undo the pressure I felt to create concrete meanings from the quiet conviction of the artist's arrangements. Frustrations such as these are what ignite the exhibition form, and I am grateful for Kimura's obdurate commitment to this way of working, one that contrasts with the poise and directness of her aesthetic attitude.

There seemed something polemical about this way of installing an exhibition. It strikes me now that the tactics of the installation move me towards some elemental question about what art, and only art, can do. Germany, at the time of the show, was still not yet fully out of its stringent laws on mask wearing and digital contact tracing protocols. This was an exhibition to be experienced in person, its studied architectural forms and spatial gamesmanship could only be unlocked by presence, which in turn could fuse into something utterly visual, and therefore, in some way, something utterly virtual. Kimura seemed to be extracting these histories of architecture and illusion to tease out some ineffable paradox perhaps best experienced in the form of an exhibition. This remains my conviction about the deep insights of this strange presentation—that it was seeking to recover a place of meaning-making from a world that had badly shaken the creative purpose and general fortitude of artists and institutions. Many artist friends seemed to be damaged by the period of pandemic isolation, most especially from a despairing sense that their artistic projects felt feeble and meaningless. So it was a relief to walk into a space that demonstrated itself so stoutly, choreographed with precision even

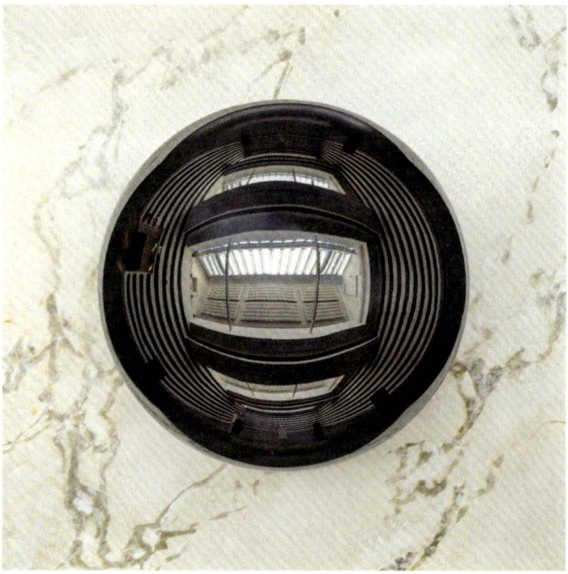

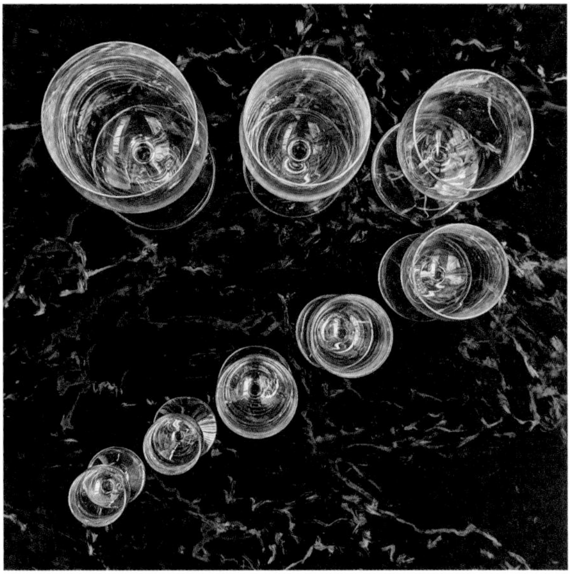

to the point of it feeling aggressively confrontational, in distinction to the rhythmic designation of negative spaces that Kimura has so often expertly factored into her past projects. Here the negative space was placed into blended balance with the geometric logics, both graphical and architectural, that fused the gallery into a more unified interdependent system of aesthetic procedures.

The quickly discovered engrossing task of finding a physical position for myself became an important and forestalling activity that I could not quit. I paced around this space, hunting the special position from which I was *meant* to see things. Kimura's works of mirror balls on plinths bounced back in concave form a reflection of the space with two figures added, those of myself and my companion that day at the Kunstverein. An irritation emerged—one familiar to life since the pandemic of "self-view" in online video calls—and that familiar split relation appeared here once more: being but also watching myself being. My body itself was the irritant to the order of things. The feeling was of being in the way, of both myself and the exhibition. I did not find the tantalizing location I had decided the work had promised me. Instead I was left to wonder about why I had mobilized my body in this precise way. An internal tension somewhere between reflection and action. Yes, this is something an exhibition (this exhibition) can (and did) do particularly well.

Remembering the exhibition from far away, it is a somatic form of memory that carries my most vivid recollection of being in that space. That feeling is something akin to motion sickness. I felt harassed by the sharp monochrome bands of paint on the walls that visually compressed the preexisting architecture into mildly psychedelic collusion with the ten plinths in its territory, tethered along carefully plotted paths that were unseeable but undoubtedly there, privately structuring the space. And if motion sickness is the experience of having travelled too far too soon, at a speed beyond our individual capacities of observation, this seems a fertile dilemma for an exhibition to contain. I am reminded of the motion sickness I so often experienced as a child. The solution, other than pulling over to vomit, was often to relegate

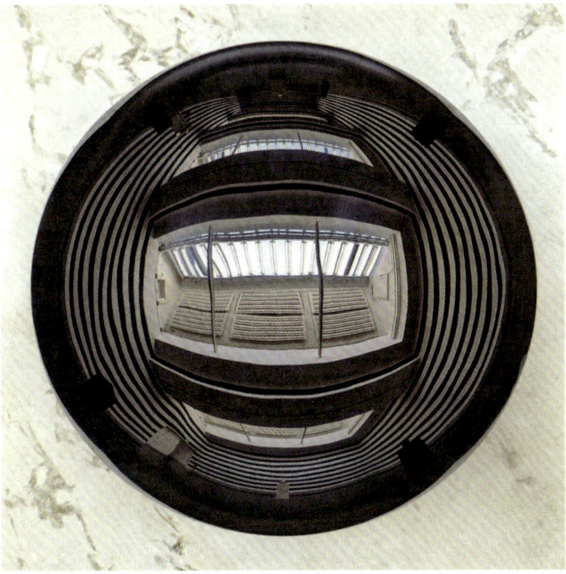

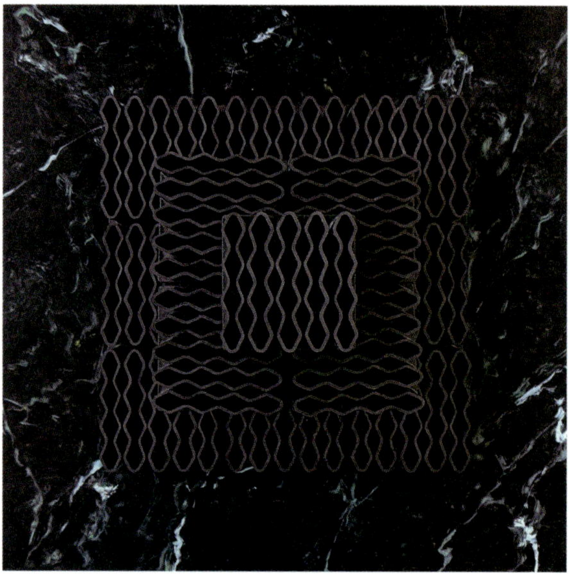

a parent to the back seat and for me to take my place in the front passenger position, where my scope of vision widened and my mind could connect the distances covered to an unfolding environment. There was secondary gain too: the oedipal triumph of forcing my father to cede to my needs so that I could sit up front with mum. The profits of Kimura's carefully fomented form of nausea were evident in how easily she tamed the handsome but daunting exhibition hall of the Kunstverein in a sweeping and refreshingly assertive treatment conspicuously free of empty devaluations of the exhibition situation itself.

On leaving the gallery, I look again at the wardrobe piece. It has not been modified or installed in the playful variations that I know from its past iterations; instead installed soberly and with a short statement available at the reception desk explaining "the artist decided not to activate the work" at a time when Russia has invaded Ukraine. It seemed an honest and uncomplicated communication about hopelessness and the de-cathecting of art's function in the face of murderous external conditions. It also illuminated

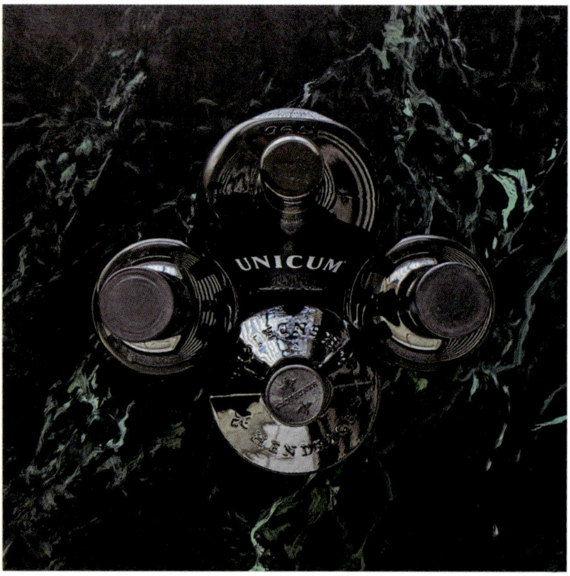
UNICUM

an important quality in the works installed in the gallery next door, most especially the importance of ambivalence to the tenor of Kimura's artistic point of address. The unambiguous pronouncement by Kimura and the Kunstverein implied that playful conceptual compositions of sculpture felt somehow impossible in light of the very recent military escalations. Let us assume, then, that the main gallery work was undertaken in a more authorized state of mind. The exhibition thrived in its balance of opposites and ambiguities. The plinths in the exhibition, for instance, were painted in trompe l'oeil style as though marble, a material prized for its natural properties and decorative colorations and veining. Something quarried from the earth here presented as façade, the chance operations of geological compression instead determined by human hand and the fine hairs of brushes. This is one of the many oscillating encounters in Kimura's exhibition between meaning and meaninglessness, emptiness and overdetermination, direction and disavowal. Ambivalence means to both love and hate at the same time, and this is an exhibition that ventured deep into an understanding that such tensile states of mind are where reality lies and where art can really begin to make demands of its environments and audiences. As I end this text, I notice the pulse of a more personal account than I had expected coming to the fore in the words I have written. This is not by chance. COL SPORCAR SI TROVA evokes a more sensual form of response because it lodged beautifully in subtle and multidetermined ways (that I have attempted to describe above) an invitation to create internal space for searching reflection. And this is achieved, perhaps counterintuitively, through a meticulous and totalizing formal treatment of the gallery. The growth of a space within me seems to be the intended cost of encountering a space that operates with clarity about how and where its own system of artistic responsibility begins and ends.

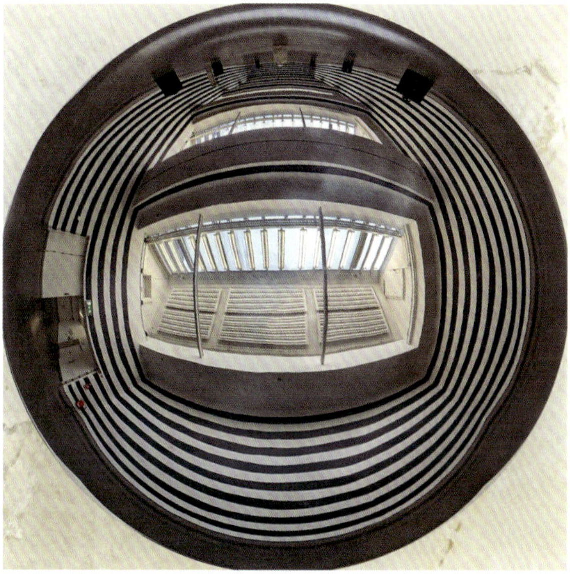

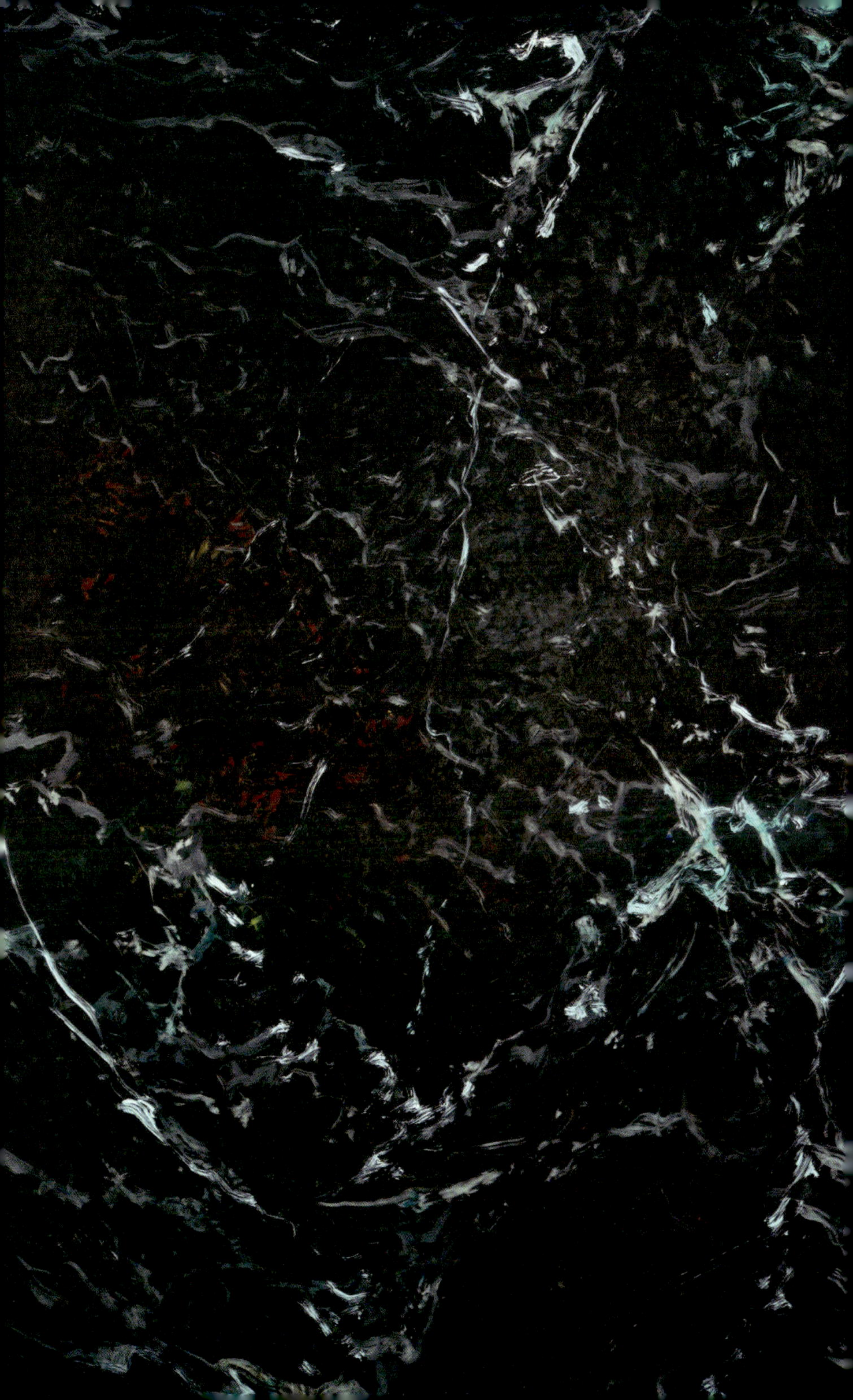

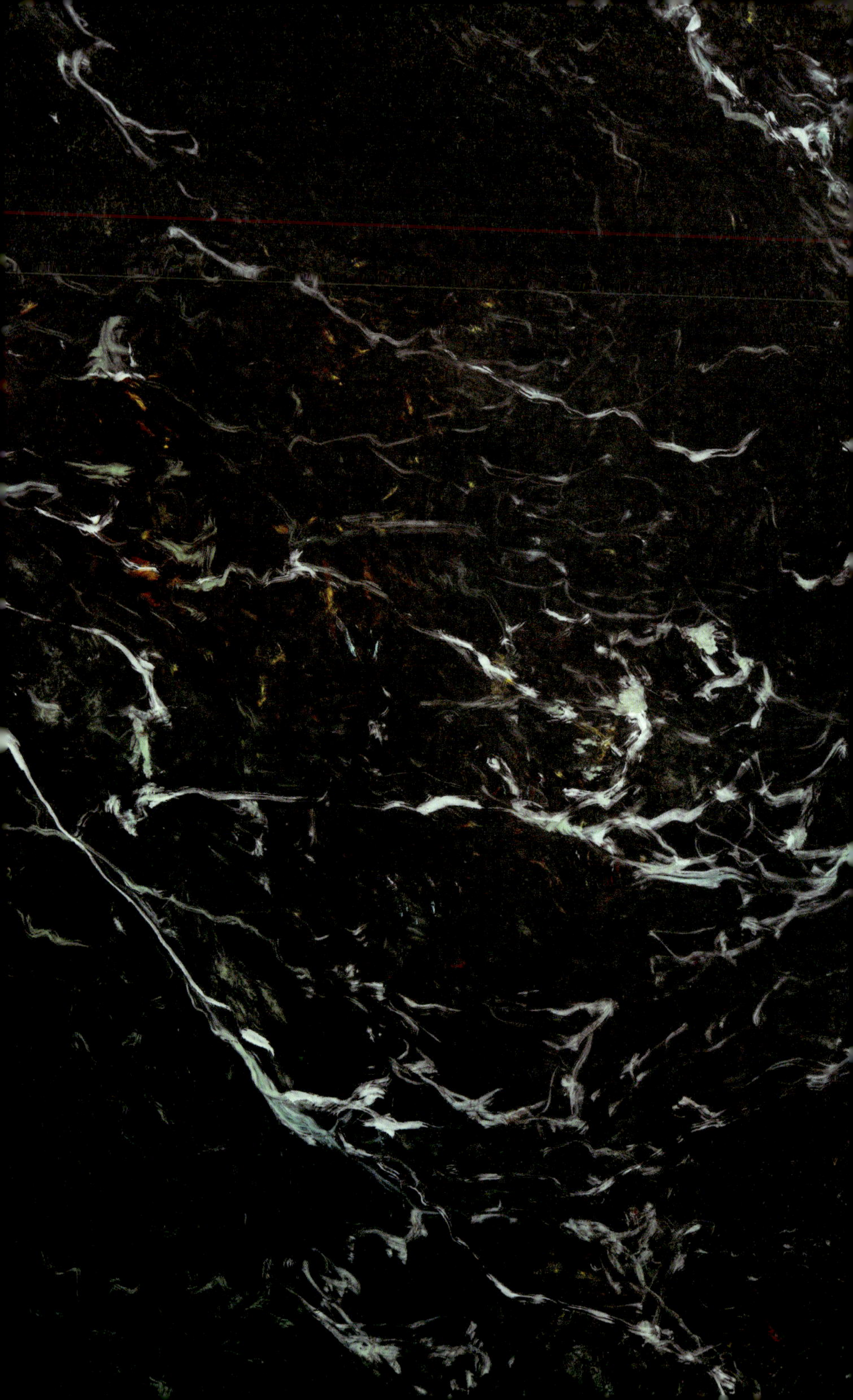

Kathrin Bentele

BY MESSING ABOUT, ONE DISCOVERS

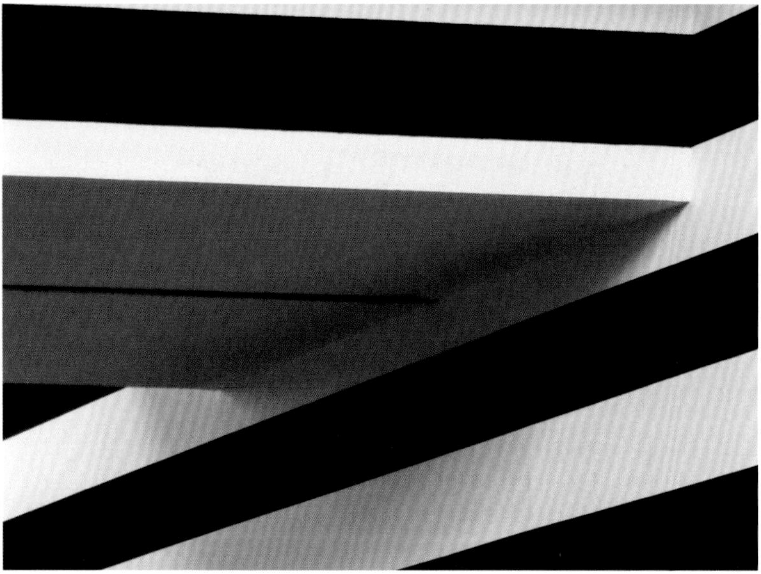

Kathrin Bentele

Yuki Kimura's work exists both as an elegant, static, physical form with a calmly assertive presence in space, and as an immaterial, wandering, and vibrating force reflective of all that exists around and throughout it—in the negative, so to speak. It initiates processes of transformation and is transformative itself, which may at first appear counterintuitive to its static appearance. The passive, mute, and durable world of objects and physical matter that one encounters in Kimura's work becomes a place of dynamic processes and shapeshifting, where the stable appearance and order of things are profoundly transformed. Kimura's work operates beyond language, occupying an entirely visual sphere, but communicates at a highly visceral and embodied level of perception.

For her exhibition at the Kunstverein für die Rheinlande und Westfalen, Düsseldorf, Kimura chooses a total formal treatment of the space that consists of a black-and-white striped painting covering all of the walls (*Stripe*), and sculptures whose plinths are covered with painted trompe l'oeil renderings of marble textures. The genesis of *Stripe* has to do with Kimura's responsiveness to the specific conditions of place and time in which she exhibits. The work developed as an attempt to over-expose and, by so doing, camouflage a salient architectural feature of the exhibition space: there are noticeable slits in the five horizontal beams that traverse the gallery's ceiling, allowing air to circulate from a concealed HVAC system stowed inside the beams. Until the end of the 1990s, this utilitarian fact was overtly shown, as the beams additionally featured ventilation grilles. The grilles were removed in the early 2000s and, in turn, replaced by the subtler slits. In hindsight, this may read as an attempt to conceal the "reality" and pragmatics of the space. Kimura's wall painting, on the contrary, is a total ornamentation that derives from that reality, even emphasizing it.

Both elements, *Stripe* and the sculptures, draw upon subtle effects of optical illusion and play, such as illusionistic alteration of volume, space, and distance by painterly means or scaling, and they invite us to experience perception as something reconciled between the mind and the body—between the metaphysical sphere of vision and the gravity of the physical world. The way in which the stripes cause the exhibition space to converge at a particular point heavily emphasizes a linear regime of sight in the disproportionally long space. Kimura's arrangement sets up a unified, hermetic, and almost virtual condition for looking, without any human touch or intentionality that indicates where to look or what to prioritize visually. Another effect of the rigid, perfectly measured backdrop is that it makes the body and everything alive and physical in the space feel inevitably registered, objectified, and measured against. A sense of non-human stasis and virtuality pervades this perfect order, as if the space had no temporality, while the viewer roams in a visual matrix whose illusionistic plays unfold with each step or turning of the head.

Like Kimura's *Mirror Ball* works displayed here, which literally call attention to optical reflection and distortion, the exhibition is deeply engaged with the dynamics of projection, reflection, inversion, mirroring, and the tension between image/vision and physicality. The notion of projection is also productive in thinking about our deep attachment to non-human matter, and to the ways in which the speechless and inert world of objects tells us something about ourselves. One of the qualities of Kimura's installation lies precisely in its ability to echo, mirror, and feed back into the life and aliveness around and throughout it, stoically and without judgment.

In a similar way, this book maintains a sense of virtuality and objectivity by removing all human intentionality from its pages. Even though the installation photographs were taken by five different people—sometimes with their own image reflected in the surfaces of *Mirror Ball*—subjective perspective is made invisible through a meticulous editing and cropping process. This process speaks to another question central to the exhibition, which concerns the erasure of human presence and the body from the long lines of modernism. A parallel may be drawn between the book's editing policy and the objective and functional grammar of architectural modernism in the West—a grammar that almost entirely eliminated the material eccentricities of decoration and ornament. By a total ornamentation of space, Kimura creates a virtual sphere of pure vision, an optical-illusionistic machinery that suspends the objective state of things for a moment.

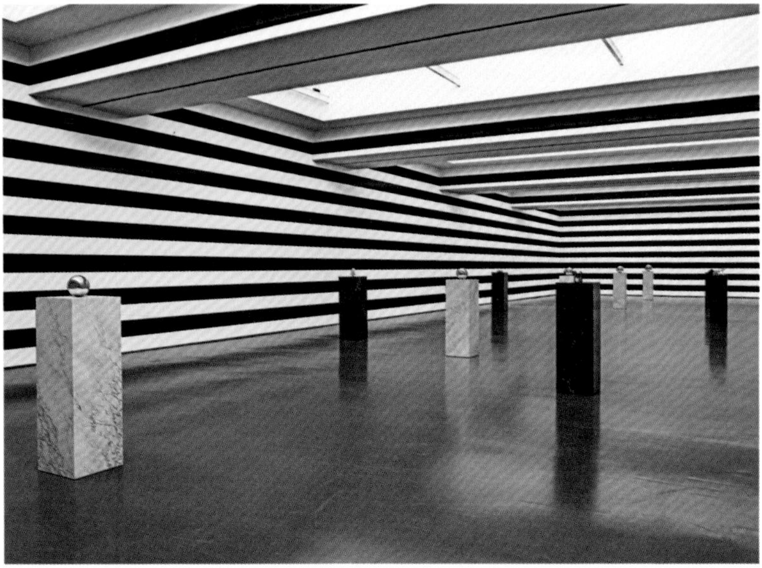

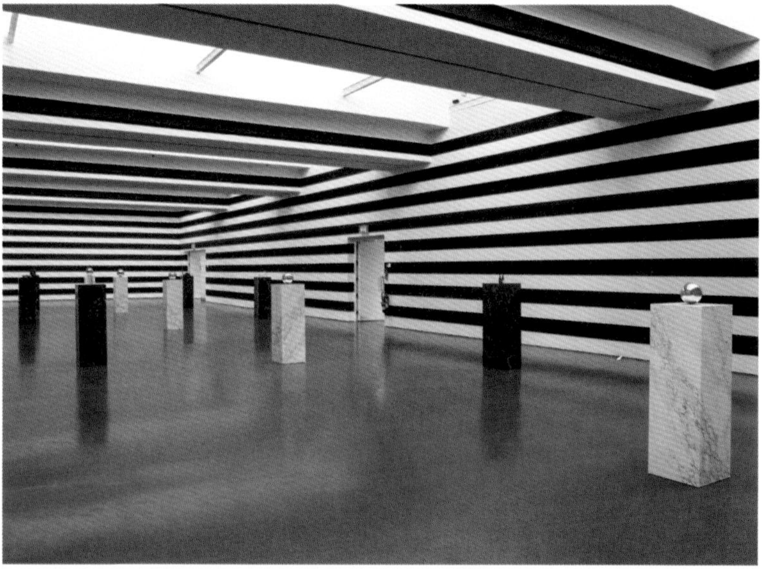

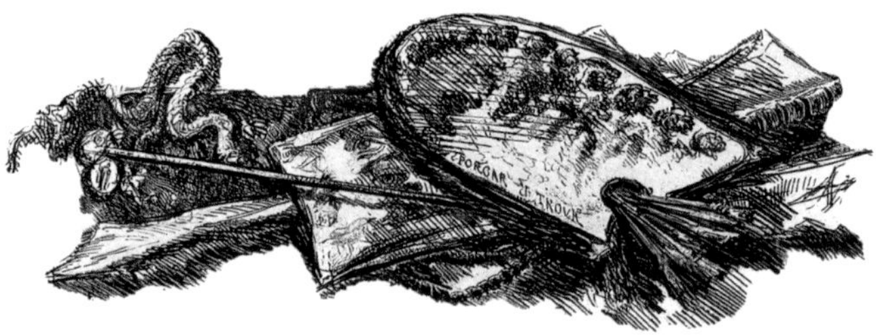

Stripe, 2022
Wall painting, black and white stripes,
450 × 3445 × 950 cm

Five Mirror Balls, 2022
Stainless steel, wood, oil paint, 150 × 40 × 40 cm /
144 × 40 × 40 cm / 140 × 40 × 40 cm / 138 × 40 × 40 cm /
135 × 40 × 40 cm

Black Bottles I, 2022
Liquor bottles, wood, oil paint, 144 × 40 × 40 cm

Black Rubber Penholders, 2022
Rubber, wood, oil paint, 132 × 40 × 40 cm

Abalones, 2022
Shells, wood, oil paint, 127.5 × 40 × 40 cm

Perfection, 2022
Glassware, wood, oil paint, 139 × 40 × 40 cm

Charms, 2022
Glassware, wood, oil paint, 139 × 40 × 40 cm

Black Bottles II, 2022
Liquor bottles, wood, oil paint, 132 × 40 × 40 cm

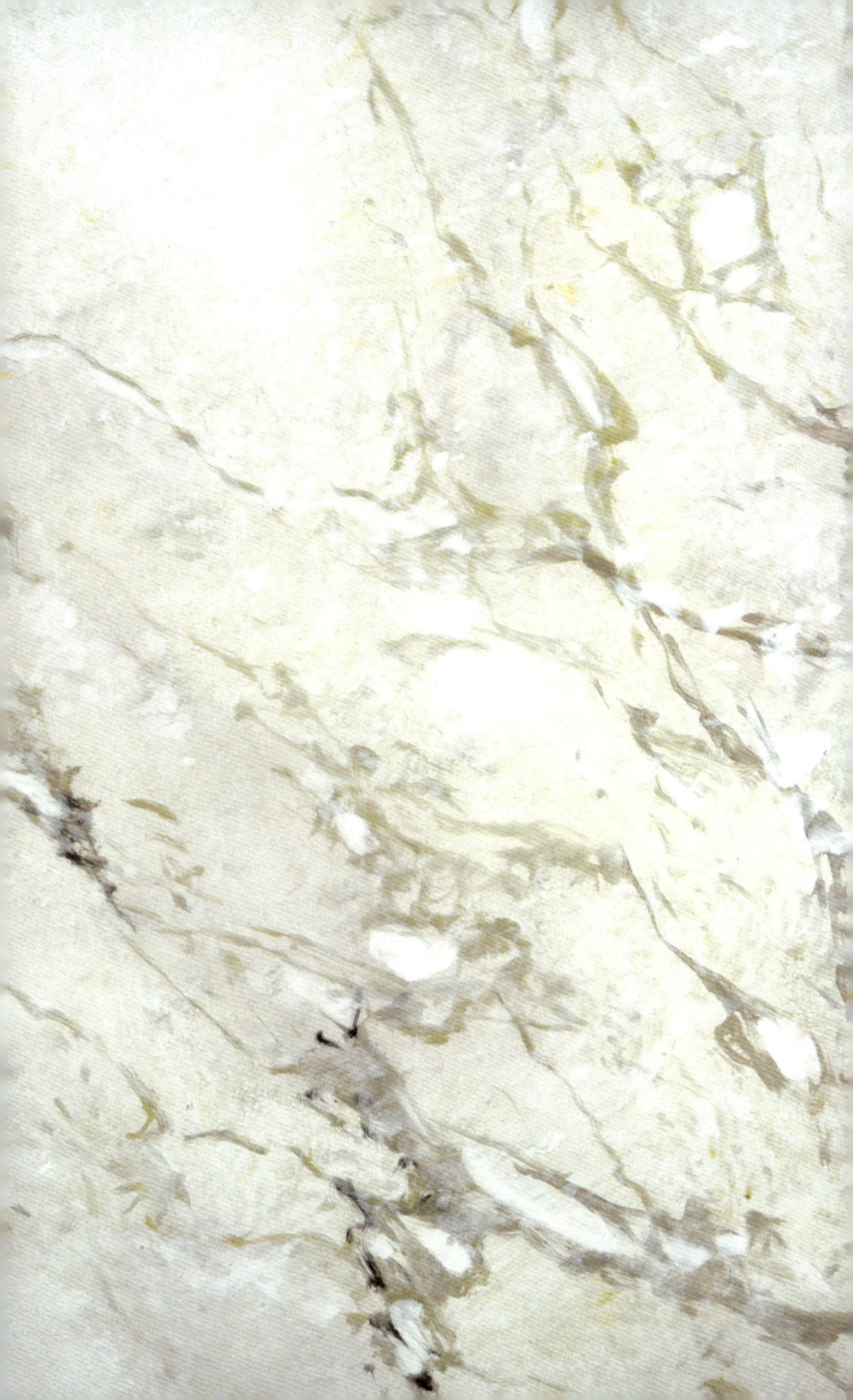

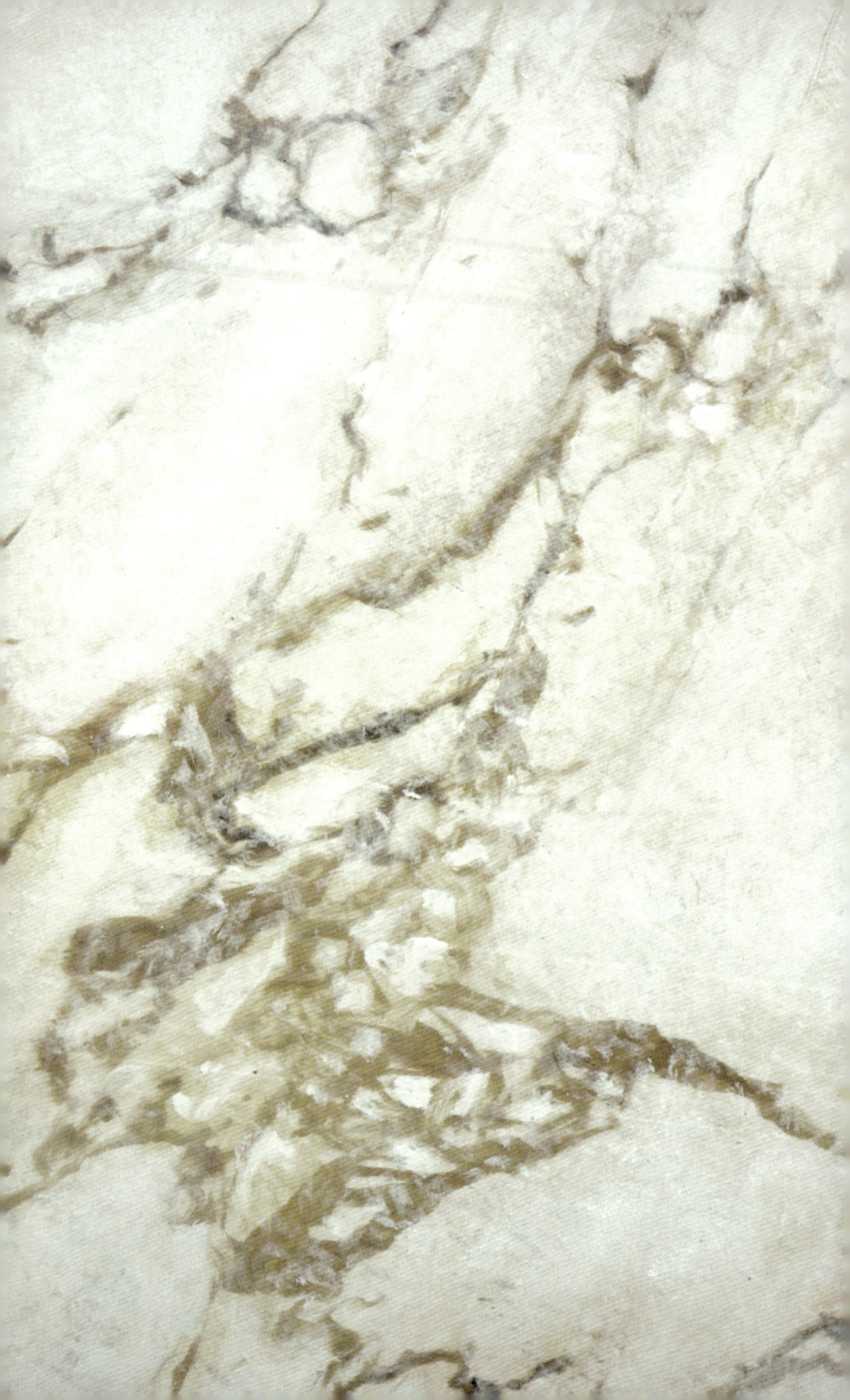

This book is published in conjunction
with the exhibition

Yuki Kimura
COL SPORCAR SI TROVA
May 14—August 21, 2022
Curated by Kathrin Bentele

Kunstverein für die Rheinlande und Westfalen,
Düsseldorf
Grabbeplatz 4, 40213 Düsseldorf
www.kunstverein-duesseldorf.de

Exhibition

Director/Curator: Kathrin Bentele
Administration/Finance: Hanna Welzel
Curatorial Assistant: Gesa Hüwe
Head of Production: Marius Comanns
Members' Services: Sigrid Konopka
Board: Lilli von Bodman, Georg Kulenkampff (Chairman), Rita McBride, Rudolf Dahmen, Ilmhart Kühn, Nicola Troydo, Renate Ulrich, Florian Wethmar

Catalogue

Editor: Kathrin Bentele
Texts: Kathrin Bentele, Jamie Stevens
Copy Editing and Proofreading: Erin Troseth
Design: Benedikt Reichenbach
Lithography: Max-Color, Berlin
Printing and binding: Medialis, Berlin
Typeface: Mercure (Charles Mazé, Abyme)
Photos: Keta Gavasheli, Yuki Kimura, Q Takeki Maeda, Cedric Mussano, Benedikt Reichenbach

Supported by

Ministerium für Kultur und Wissenschaft des Landes Nordrhein-Westfalen

公益財団法人 ポーラ美術振興財団 POLA ART FOUNDATION

JAPANFOUNDATION

Landeshauptstadt Düsseldorf

Stadtwerke Düsseldorf

Taka Ishii Gallery

GALERIE CHANTAL CROUSEL

The artist would like to thank

Sylvie Van der Kelen, Kazuhiro Yajima, Peter Lenz, Josef Paulis, Norihito Nakatani, Kazuna Taguchi, Soshiro Matsubara, Rodney and Taka Nonaka-Hill, Takayuki Mashiyama, Q Takeki Maeda

Published and distributed by

Mousse Publishing
Contrappunto S.r.l.
Via Pier Candido Decembrio 28
20137, Milan

Available through:
Mousse Publishing, Milan
www.moussemagazine.it
DAP | Distributed Art Publishers, New York
www.artbook.com
Les presses du réel, Dijon
www.lespressesdureel.com
Antenne Books, London
www.antennebooks.com

Giovanni Battista Piranesi, detail of frontispiece of *Raccolta di alcuni disegni del Barbieri da Cento detto il Guercino*, 1764: © Alamy (Page 101)

Printed in Germany
ISBN 978-88-6749-579-5
€27 / $30